P9-CFZ-545
3 2109 00779 2816

Mothers and Daughters in American Short Fiction

Recent Titles in
Bibliographies and Indexes in Women's Studies

Psychological and Medical Aspects of Induced Abortion: A Selective, Annotated Bibliography, 1970-1986
Eugenia B. Winter, compiler

Women Writers of Germany, Austria, and Switzerland: An Annotated Bio-Bibliographical Guide
Elke Frederiksen, editor

Immigrant Women in the United States: A Selectively Annotated Multidisciplinary Bibliography
Donna Gabaccia, compiler

Women and the Literature of the Seventeenth Century: An Annotated Bibliography Based on Wing's *Short Title Catalogue*
Hilda Smith and Susan Cardinale, compilers

Women and Mass Communications: An International Annotated Bibliography
John A. Lent

Sources on the History of Women's Magazines, 1792-1960: An Annotated Bibliography
Mary Ellen Zuckerman, compiler

Feminist Research Methods: An Annotated Bibliography
Connie Miller with Corinna Treitel

War and Peace through Women's Eyes: A Selective Bibliography of Twentieth-Century American Women's Fiction
Susanne Carter

American Women Playwrights, 1900-1930: A Checklist
Frances Diodato Bzowski, compiler

Women in Japanese Society: An Annotated Bibliography of Selected English Language Materials
Kristina Ruth Huber, with Kathryn Sparling

United States Government Documents on Women, 1800-1990: A Comprehensive Bibliography, Volume I: Social Issues
Mary Ellen Huls

United States Government Documents on Women, 1800-1990: A Comprehensive Bibliography, Volume II: Labor
Mary Ellen Huls

Mothers and Daughters in American Short Fiction

An Annotated Bibliography of Twentieth-Century Women's Literature

Compiled by
Susanne Carter

Bibliographies and Indexes in Women's Studies, Number 19

Greenwood Press
Westport, Connecticut • London

Library of Congress Cataloging-in-Publication Data

Carter, Susanne.
Mothers and daughters in American short fiction : an annotated bibliography of twentieth-century women's literature / compiled by Susanne Carter.
p. cm.—(Bibliographies and indexes in women's studies, ISSN 0742-6941 ; no. 19)
Includes indexes.
ISBN 0-313-28511-X (alk. paper)
1. Short stories, American—Women authors—Bibliography. 2. Women and literature—United States—Bibliography. 3. Mothers and daughters in literature—Bibliography. 4. American fiction—20th century—Bibliography. I. Title. II. Series.
Z1229.W8C37 1993
[PS374.W6]
016.813'01083520431—dc20 93-10822

British Library Cataloguing in Publication Data is available.

Library of Congress Catalog Card Number: 93-10822
ISBN: 0-313-28511-X
ISSN: 0742-6941

First published in 1993

Greenwood Press, 88 Post Road West, Westport, CT 06881
An imprint of Greenwood Publishing Group, Inc.

Printed in the United States of America

The paper used in this book complies with the Permanent Paper Standard issued by the National Information Standards Organization (Z39.48-1984).

10 9 8 7 6 5 4 3 2 1

To the Women's Reading Circle

Contents

Preface

This bibliography is the result of an effort to compile and analyze short fiction written by American women during the twentieth century which explores the mother-daughter relationship. The 242 stories included in the bibliography have been divided thematically into seven chapters: Abuse and Neglect, Aging, Alienation, Death, Expectations, Nurturance, and Portraits. Each chapter begins with an introductory overview and collective analysis of the stories included in that chapter. Annotations offering a critical summary of each short story pertaining to the particular chapter's theme follows, concluded by a list of sources cited within that chapter, where applicable.

Each individual citation of the bibliography has been numbered and includes complete bibliographic information presented in the format of the MLA Handbook for Writers of Research Papers (Third Edition, 1988). Quotations included within individual annotations have been referenced according to MLA standards as well. The author and title indices at the end of the book reference these citations by number. The subject index references citations by item number and introductory pages of each chapter by page number.

Acknowledgments

I would like to express my gratitude to the following people who assisted me in the research for this bibliography: the interlibrary loan staff of Southwest Missouri State University, the editorial and voluntary staff members of Calyx, the editorial staff of Iowa Woman, the editor and indexing staff of Short Story Index. I also wish to thank the members of the Women's Reading Circle, where this idea originated.

Introduction

In 1976 Adrienne Rich brought to awareness the silence that for many years had surrounded "the most formative relationship in the life of every woman, the relationship between daughter and mother" (Hirsch 200). In her classic feminist work, Of Woman Born: Motherhood as Experience and Institution, Rich described the mother-daughter bond as the "great unwritten story" that awaited analysis and definition. She wrote:

> This cathexis between mother and daughter—essential, distorted, misused—is the great unwritten story. Probably there is nothing in human nature more resonant with charges than the flow of energy between two biologically alike bodies, one of which has lain in amniotic bliss inside the other, one of which has labored to give birth to the other. The materials are here for the deepest mutuality and the most painful estrangement. (225 – 226)

Mother-daughter relationships have been historically ignored, even by mothers and daughters themselves, because of the ways women consciously and unconsciously think of themselves and others, Signe Hammer explains in her Introduction to Daughters and Mothers: Mothers and Daughters (xiii). In Western cultural tradition, she writes, "we have viewed relationships from a masculine perspective; women have been considered important only in terms of their roles as the wives and mothers of men" (xiii). Because women have been identified by society as primarily wives and mothers, and daughters as potential wives and mothers, Hammer points out, it has been difficult for mothers and daughters to see themselves or each other as separate individuals (xiii). Only recently through the combined influences of feminism and contemporary psychology has the concept of "self " emerged as an idea that is "common to all people, both male and female" (xiii).

Since the silence surrounding the mother-daughter relationship was first revealed by Rich, "many voices have come to fill this gap, to create speech and meaning where there has been silence and absence," Marianne Hirsch writes in her review essay "Mothers and Daughters" (201). During the past two decades, the voices of sociologists, psychologists, feminist scholars, historians, artists, poets, novelists, and short story writers have blended together in common exploration of the "great unwritten story," their interpretations of the mother-daughter bond shaped and reshaped by current feminist thought. For there can be no comprehensive study of womanhood, Hirsch states, that "does not take into account woman's role as a mother of daughters and as a daughter of mothers, that does not study female identity in relation to previous and subsequent generations of women, and that does not study that relationship in the wider context in which it takes place: the emotional, political, economic, and symbolic structures of family and society. Any study of mother-daughter relationships, Hirsch contends, becomes both feminist and interdisciplinary" (202).

The once silenced subject of mother-daughter relationships has become a common theme in contemporary fiction authored by American women. Novels such as Amy Tan's The Joy Luck Club, Gail Godwin's A Mother and Two Daughters, Toni Morrison's The Bluest Eye, Mona Simpson's Anywhere But Here, and Sue Miller's The Good Mother have openly and candidly explored many of the issues which concern mothers and daughters. As the 242 stories included in this bibliography indicate, short story writers too have added their literary voices to those who are continuing to examine and reexamine the many-faceted and often complex bond between mothers and daughters. These stories offer insight into not only traditional American mother-daughter relationships, but also Native American, Norwegian-American, Chinese-American, Japanese-American, Jewish, and Black mother-daughter relationships as well.

Novels and short stories which "candidly recount the lives of mothers and daughters," writes Shelly Phillips in Beyond the Myths: Mother-Daughter Relationships in Psychology, History, Literature and Everyday Life, "often reflect our own lives" (164). These reflections can help us to better understand ourselves as women who are mothers and daughters and our relationships with one another. Accurate literary portrayals of mother-daughter relationships and the inevitable conflicts that accompany this intimate relationships can be beneficial as a cathartic bibliotherapy for women seeking to better understand themselves (Phillips 164). Contemporary women writers are endeavoring to "rework, rethink, rediscover and establish a positive context for mother-daughter relationships," writes Phillips. She elaborates:

> There is a growing literature which is reflecting and confirming mother-daughter experiences in a way that is relevant and cathartic. It is a validating literature which depicts a great range of genuine mother-daughter experience. Its images are ones in which mothers and daughters can find their own identity. Through these images they can know that their experiences of each other have been shared by other women. (164)

The American fictional interpretations of the 192 women writers included in this bibliography are varied and often strikingly dissimilar. For instance, the mother in Rachel Simon's "Breath of This Night" asks each of her three young daughters to breathe into individual jars so that she might preserve their special essences forever. In contrast, the demands of mothering two daughters prove to be so radically different from the romantic perception of motherhood once nurtured by the young mother in Sheila Kohler's "A Quiet Place" that she dreams her younger daughter is drowning, awakening in a frightened state of panic that perhaps her subconscious dream has come true. In Fatima Shaid's "Before Echo" a mother abandons her young daughter at birth, escaping from the Louisiana swamplands to the streets of New Orleans where she sells her body for a living until years later she decides to attempt motherhood for the first time after being reunited with her adolescent daughter. The Chinese-American mother in Amy Tan's "Two

Kinds" attempts to mold her young daughter into a child prodigy while the mother in Jean McCord's "I Left It All Behind When I Ran" hopes her daughter will become the artist she always wanted to be. The single, black mother in Shirley Ann Grau's "The Beginning" empowers her daughter with a sense of self-respect and infinite possibility worthy of a princess at an early age so that by the time she learns that she is an illegitimate black woman, she is beyond vulnerability and full of self-assuredness. In contrast, the mothernarrator of Tillie Olsen's "I Stand Here Ironing" can only hope her adolescent daughter will escape the stigma of her background and not simply become an extension of her own poverty and disappointment. But the poor mother speaking to her daughter in Jamaica Kincaid's "Girl" who is teaching her daughter the necessary skills to survive on the streets, offers no such hope that her daughter will someday be able to break the confines of poverty.

Between mothers and daughters there exists an "extraordinary bond," writes Ruth J. Moss in her essay "Generations of Images." "Whether it is cherished or despised the bond endures" (80). Even into old age, the entanglement between mothers and daughters continues as mothers struggle to satisfy the demands of their daughters while daughters continue to perform duties for their mothers in order to retain the approval and affection they need from one another (Pildes 7). Thus, while the adult daughter in Florence Chanock Cohen's "The Golden Triangle" tries in vain to prove her aging mother sane enough to gain admittance into an exclusive hotel for the elderly, the daughter in Mary Jane Moffat's "Giving My Mother a Bath" carefully washes the fragile, wrinkled body of her mother that is gradually deteriorating. As these and other stories illustrate, a reversal of roles often occurs as mothers age and become more dependent, while their daughters assume the traditional maternal responsibilities of their mothers.

The power that mothers wield over their daughters continues, even as mothers age and their minds and bodies begin to fail. But mothers still retain the ability to manipulate and control their daughters' lives, this literature clearly illustrates. The mother-daughter relationship fictionalized in Corinne Demas Bliss's "Small Sins" provides an excellent example of maternal power. The aging but crafty mother in this story carefully schemes to get her way until her daughter is left with no other alternative but to forsake her better judgment and reluctantly invite her mother to move in with her family.

In her essay "Mother's Day: Bittersweet" Martha Weinman Lear suggests that as mothers age, their identities merge with their daughters' in a "murderous entanglement" that is passed on from generation to generation of women. She writes:

> Liberation. Extrication. Our mothers grow old and we watch them becoming us, and ourselves becoming them, and whom do we extricate from what? And how? And do we pass this dear, murderous entanglement on to our daughters with the family silver? Often I wonder if this is not some ultimate form of liberation: the most painful and the most elusive. (13)

In the preface to her story "Rules of the Game," Amy Tan characterizes mothers as their daughters' "greatest ally and adversary." While more maternal adversaries than allies appear in the pages of the short stories included in this bibliography, evidence of both roles exists. Mothers and daughters are inherently natural allies as well as natural enemies,

Victoria Secunda explains further in When You and Your Mother Can't Be Friends. "No relationship is as highly charged as that between mother and daughter," she writes, "or as riddled with expectations that could, like a land mine, detonate with a single misstep, a solitary stray word that, without warning, wounds or enrages. And no relationship is as bursting with possibilities of goodwill and understanding" (5). A similar analysis of the ambivalent mother-daughter bond is presented by Geri Giebel Chavis in Family: Stories From the Interior. "Deep affection fuses with bitter resentment," she explains, "as mothers and daughters take care of one another, focus on their mutual expectations, and struggle to clarify boundaries" (52).

"The first knowledge any woman has of warmth, nourishment, tenderness, security, sensuality, mutuality, comes from mother," writes Jacquelyn F. Douglass in her dissertation, "A Study of Literature of Mother-Daughter Relationships as it Relates to Self-Esteem of the Adult Daughter." "That earliest entrapment of one female body with another can sooner or later be denied or rejected, felt as choking possessiveness, as rejection, trap, or taboo; but it is, at the beginning, the whole world" (66). The relationship that mothers and daughters share "affects women profoundly at all stages of their lives," Hammer's research has proven (xi). Even if not all women become mothers during their lifetimes, they remain daughters all of their lives. And the transition from daughterhood to motherhood "remains the central rite of passage in the lives of women, as it has been throughout history" (4).

Daughters learn how to be women from the most powerful role models present in their lives—their mothers—who both consciously and unconsciously teach their daughters what women are (Pildes 5). "As the first mirror of life and the world," writes Douglass, "mother serves as guide, protector and interpreter through the maze of womanhood and our culture" (21). She continues:

> Our first sense of self is as an extension of mother, and the struggle for autonomy and independence lies in the eternal conflict of this symbiotic bond and the will toward oneness. Through this mother stands as a lasting model and a touchstone in our lives. (21)

While daughters continue to imitate and identify with their mothers as they age, Chavis explains, their mothers "invariably see reflections of their younger selves in their daughters" (52). "Mothers tend to be invested in the lives of their daughters," she writes, "since they expect their daughters to experience joys and sorrows similar to their own and often seek to fulfill their unrealized dreams through their daughters' opportunities" (52). When a mother and daughter have no connection, the daughter loses her primary role model and is left on her own to figure out the experiences of womanhood. "Such a daughter," writes Secunda, "has to discover herself, alone" (6). This is the unfortunate fate of the daughter in Jelena Bulat Gill's "Nobody Under the Rose" who resorts to prostitution and allows herself to be abused because she grew up deprived of maternal nurturing.

Although daughters may strive to be independent as they grow up, they continue to need their mothers' approval and support. "We want to survive," explains Secunda "but not entirely without her. We want to detach, but not defect. Because, like it or not, we are still very much bound up with her" (6) Secunda describes the special need that continues to bond daughters to their mothers, even into adulthood:

> Whether our relationship is strained or easy, hostile or amiable, we need her, if only in memory or fantasy, to conjugate our history, validate our femaleness, and guide our way; we need to know she's there if we stumble, to love us no matter what, to nurture the child that resides within us even now without infantilizing us. It is a need that never leaves us in the best of mother-daughter attachments and, in the worst, yawns wider than the heart can bear. (6)

Short stories written by Helen Schulman and Jamaica Kincaid support Secunda's premise on mother-daughter bonding. The daughter who narrates Kincaid's "My Mother" expresses a sense of peace as she walks along with her mother, the two of them seeming to blend together as the daughter confides that "I could not see where she left off and I began, or where I left off and she began" (97). The daughter in Schulman's "Not a Free Show" who fears she will not be able to survive after her mother's death admits,"I do not know where I end and she begins again" (143).

Although our mothers are our primary role models and our own standard of comparison for evaluating ourselves, many daughters consciously try to be different from their mothers. Whatever faults we find in our mothers, we invariably begin to suspect that these are blemishes in ourselves as well. Deprecation of our mothers can lead to self-deprecation of ourselves as daughters. So while daughters strive determinedly to be different, at the same time "we often have an almost superstitious belief that we simply *cannot* avoid that repetition. We secretly fear that we are exactly like our mothers in all the ways that we dislike" (Caplan 31). This tendency is exemplified by the daughter-protagonist of Anais Nin's "A Slippery Floor" who bases her career choice and lifestyle on her deliberate vow "to be as unlike my mother as possible," even though her mother has been a distant stranger most of her life.

Mother-daughter relationships vary greatly. While some of the mothers and daughters characterized in these stories maintain close, compassionate relationships until parted by death, still others remain alienated, embittered, and frustrated with one another throughout their lives. While some mothers nurture, protect, and support their daughters, others abuse, neglect, and ignore theirs. While some mothers grant their daughters freedom of choice and individuality, others attempt to control their daughters' lives even into adulthood. "Even within the same family," Lucy Fischer maintains in Linked Lives: Adult Daughters and Their Mothers, "a mother may have different kinds of relationships with each of several daughters. If there is so much variability within the same family," she explains further, "we can assume that there is even more diversity in expectations for mothers and daughters across cultures, societies, and historical periods" (196).

Fischer concludes from her mother-daughter research that transformations in family structure greatly affect mother-daughter relationships. As daughters grow up and become mothers themselves, inevitable changes reshape the mother-daughter bond. While mothers and daughters often become like peers in some ways, at the same time they retain their roles as parents and children. Family roles place opposing demands on both daughters and mothers who are alternately "pulled together and pushed apart" (197). The newly married daughter and her once close mother in Tess Slesinger's "Mother to Dinner" are victims of this conflict in roles. The daughter in this story confesses that she feels like a "human shuttle" vacillating between her husband and mother, unable to be both wife and daughter since her affection has been divided between two people.

Cultural influences often shape mother-daughter relationships. The control that Chinese-American mothers wield over their daughters is exemplified over and over again in Amy Tan's novels and short stories. In a Chinese family, Tan explains in Inter/View:Talks with America's Writing Women, a daughter does not have permission to think a new idea of her own until her mother decides to plant it in her mind. As she was growing up, she remembers that " 'the notion of never being independent from my mother was so terrifying to me that I went to extremes to sever (the bond)' " that now, as an adult, she is still trying to " 'pull tighter' " again (16).

Societal changes also influence the relationships of mothers and daughters. Women today who belong to the post-war Baby Boom generation probably have less in common with their mothers than any two generations of women in history, Secunda proposes (61). "The whole notion of what it means to be a woman has stood on its head" during the last quarter of the century, leaving mothers feeling alienated from the "unfamiliar terrain" of their daughters' lives. The confines which once prescribed their own lives as women and mothers have disappeared (Secunda 61). No longer do women define themselves solely by spouses and children but by careers in almost every field and their individual endeavors. Notions of motherhood, too, have changed during the maturation of this generation. No longer does a woman feel obligated to be married in order to give birth to a child; in fact, through artificial insemination the concept of father has been reduced to an anonymous semen donor. Many women, by choice or as the result of divorce, are raising sons and daughters by themselves. No longer do women feel they must turn to motherhood for fulfillment. Still others have developed lesbian relationships, with or without children. And when a daughter has problems, she does not automatically turn to her mother for solace. Self-help groups and a myriad of therapy alternatives have frequently replaced the need for a mother's compassionate ear and words of advice.

Mothers who matured during the 1970s women's movement have added challenges raising their daughters, as explained in Ann F. Caron's "Don't Stop Loving Me." These women have the responsibility to guide their daughters through a different environment than they—or their mothers—experienced. For these mothers, there are few guidelines; they are pathfinders in an ever-changing society with different expectations of women. While they may be confident that their daughters will benefit from increased opportunities, they are haunted by traditional fears that plague all mothers of adolescent females, including not only the "old worry" of unwanted pregnancy but newer "specters" of drug and alcohol abuse, rape, and eating disorders. Caron explains this challenge many women face:

> They do not want to shackle their daughters, yet they wonder about their daughters' ability to meet the demands placed upon them. They vacillate between their daughters' need for independence and need for safety. They want their daughters to develop into women who can handle everything, but they hesitate because there seem to be so many dangers out there.
>
> Above all, they long to share their lives while respecting their individualities. As women know from their own relationship with their mothers, this closeness can be suffocating or it can be liberating. The right balance does not happen automatically. It must be worked on. (5)

While these recent societal trends have permanently altered traditional roles of women and have changed the nature of mother-daughter relationships, they have created some very positive benefits for women. As we approach the end of the century, many daughters are growing up with the idea that motherhood is an option, not an obligation, and that women who choose not to become mothers can still retain their identities as individuals. As models of independence and self-sufficiency who are much more open about the concept of womanhood with their daughters than their mothers were with them, many women are successfully empowering their daughters "with a strong sense of themselves as persons who are women," a consciousness which will undoubtedly be passed on to their own daughters as the mother-daughter bond continues to be shaped and reshaped by successive generations of women (Hammer, Introduction xvi)

Sources:

Caplan, Paula J. Don't Blame Mother: Mending the Mother-Daughter Relationship. New York: Harper and Row, 1989.

Caron, Ann F. "Don't Stop Loving Me." New York: Henry Holt, 1991.

Chavis, Geri Giebel, ed. Family: Stories from the Interior. St. Paul: Graywolf Press, 1987.

Davidson, Cathy N. and E. M. Broner. The Lost Tradition: Mothers and Daughters in Literature. New York: Frederick Ungar, 1980.

Douglass, Jacquelyn F. "A Study of Literature of Mother-Daughter Relationships as it Relates to Self-Esteem of the Adult Daughter." Diss. Temple University, 1988.

Fischer, Lucy Rose. Linked Lives: Adult Daughters and Their Mothers. New York: Harper and Row, 1986.

Godwin, Gail. A Mother and Two Daughters. New York: Viking Press, 1982.

Hammer, Signe. Daughters and Mothers: Mothers and Daughters. New York: New York Times Book Company, 1975.

Hirsch, Marianne. "Review Essay: Mothers and Daughters." Signs: Journal of Women in Culture and Society. 7.1 (1981) 200 – 222.

Lear, Martha Weinman. "Mother's Day: Bittersweet." New York Times Magazine 11 May 1975: 13.

Miller, Sue. The Good Mother. New York: Harper and Row, 1986.

Morrison, Toni. The Bluest Eye. New York: Holt, Rinehart, and Winston, 1970.

Pearlman, Mickey and Katerine Usher Henderson. Inter/View: Talks with America's Writing Women. Lexington: University Press of Kentucky, 1990.

Phillips, Shelley. Beyond the Myths: Mother-Daughter Relationships in Psychology, History, Literature, and Everyday Life. Sydney: Hampden Press, 1991.

Pildes, Judith. "Mothers and Daughters: Understanding the Roles." Frontiers. 3.2 (1978) 2 – 11.

Rich, Adrienne. Of Woman Born: Motherhood as Experience and Institution. New York: W. W. Norton and Company, 1976.

Secunda, Victoria. When You and Your Mother Can't Be Friends. New York: Delacorte Press, 1990.

Simpson, Mona. Anywhere But Here. New York: Knopf, 1986.

Tan, Amy. The Joy Luck Club. New York: Putnam's, 1989.

Mothers and Daughters in American Short Fiction

1

Abuse and Neglect

INTRODUCTION

The mother-daughter bond does not always create a close and loving relationship. Beginning motherhood frequently causes conflict and tension for women who are unprepared to become mothers or incapable of accepting the responsibilities involved. The result is that mothers sometimes abandon, neglect, and abuse their daughters both emotionally and physically, as these stories illustrate.

For some of these women, motherhood is merely an interference in their lives, an intrusion upon their preoccupation with their own needs and interests. For other women, their personal problems are too consuming of their time and energy to allow them to nurture a child. Daughters in Molly Best Tinsley's "Zoe," Susan Neville's "The Invention of Flight," Jelena Bulat Gill's "Nobody Under the Rose," Amy Hempel's "Tom-Rock Through the Eels," Daphne Patai's "On Your Fifty-fifth Birthday," and Audrey Thomas's "Real Mothers" all suffer the emotional consequences of maternal neglect. Following her mother's suicide, the daughter in Hempel's "Tom-Rock Through the Eels" sleeps in the bed where her mother's dead body lay, hoping to remember the few "good times" she had with her mother. But all of her memories are of the mothers of her friends, who showed obvious signs of love for their daughters, unlike her own mother who "wore me like a fur" and never attempted to cultivate a close relationship. The divorced mother in Audrey Thomas's "Real Mothers," who distances herself emotionally from her daughters (even requesting that they call her by her first name) when she takes a live-in lover, realizes her neglect of her daughters too late, for they have already chosen to live with their father instead. Neville's story is narrated by an observer living in the same house with a mother and her adult daughter who observes the mother's obvious neglect of the daughter and the resulting unhappiness it causes. "The mother is so happy and the daughter in such obvious misery," the narrator writes, "that I am convinced the mother has in some way made Melissa the way that she is, that it is she who is completely responsible for what Melissa has become, as if she gave birth to her to absorb her spirit; I am certain there is no love between them" (95).

Daughters characterized in Anne Moody's "The Cow" and Joyce Carol Oates's "The Children" also suffer physical abuse at the hands of their mothers. To the mother in Moody's story, the birth of her daughter is yet another event in the series of unfortunate circumstances which have characterized her young life. Although Truelove beats her daughter, it does not cure Louella's innate stubbornness; neither does it change the poverty and misery which characterize Truelove's fate in life. Oates's story indicates that even mothers with the best of intentions toward motherhood also have the potential for abuse. The young mother in Oates's story also becomes physically abusive when motherhood turns out to be a very different experience than she had anticipated. Devoting her energies exclusively to mothering once she gives birth to her daughter, Ginny's perceptions become limited and distorted by her narrowed vision of life. When a second child is born, she misinterprets her daughter's natural jealousy of her newborn brother as potentially threatening to her son's life and lashes out violently at her daughter in defense of him. It is her own misdirected anger and frustration at her disappointment with motherhood that are the driving forces behind this mother's abusive treatment of her daughter.

Their addiction to alcohol forms a barrier that prevents mothers from building close relationships with their daughters in short stories authored by Deborah Slosberg, Joyce Carol Oates, and Joy Williams. All three daughters in these stories grow up without the assurance of maternal love and suffer from neglect and embarrassment that stems from their mothers' addictions. The poor black mother and her daughter in Sauda Jamal's "A Mother That Loves You" share a mutual addiction to drugs and stealing as a way of life, the mother congratulating her daughter on her ability to "hustle" at the youthful age of 14.

In only one of these stories is there hope given that a mother-daughter relationship may survive obvious maternal neglect. Although the mother in Fatima Shaid's "Before Echo" abandoned her daughter at birth, leaving her in the Louisiana swamp while she sold her body on the streets of New Orleans to make a living, once they are reunited she decides to return to the swamp to live and begin a relationship for the first time with her adolescent daughter.

SHORT FICTION

1. Bradley, Jane. "Noises." Power Lines and Other Stories. Fayetteville: University of Arkansas Press, 1989. 90 – 101.

   The adult daughter in this story follows the same pattern set by her mother as she becomes an abused wife, just as her mother was. Although Connie offers her daughter an asylum from the abuse of her sometimes volatile husband, even taking up arms to physically protest her daughter from his wrath, Trisha rejects the "safe love" her mother offers and returns to uncertain love in a potentially dangerous relationship. She returns to a man who plays the same game she remembers her father playing—"the black turn game"— in which a "man could be happy as a prince until you said the wrong word, made the wrong sound that could make a man in love swoop like a hawk ready to grab anything that dared to move across the ground" (92). Jimbo echoes the same words Trisha often heard her father scream at her mother—" 'You asked for it!' " (92). All of the protective maternal instincts against dangers Connie remembers feeling when her daughter was an infant return now that her daughter is again in need of security and compassion. But Trisha accepts her mother's offer of protective refuge only long enough to regain her physical and mental strength before she returns to her husband, despite her mother's warnings, choosing abusive love over maternal love.

2. Braverman, Kate. "Winter Blues." Squandering the Blue. New York: Fawcett Columbine, 1990. 17 – 33.

A single mother bears the enormity of the task of parenting her young daughter alone while she works toward earning a teaching degree in this story. Learning the art of reading a textbook while she dresses Barbie and sponges up spilled milk, Erica attempts to juggle the two roles of mother and student but not without the frustration of feeling as if she is constantly slighting one or the other. As a mother torn between conflicting roles, "she has learned to give the appearance of being physically present when in fact she is somewhere else entirely. Or perhaps this is a kind of emotional sleight of hand she always knew. Perhaps it is a rare, intrinsic gift, something she was born with" (20). It is fitting that the very week Erica and her daughter are trapped indoors by winter rains and power outages and she has exhausted all creative attempts at keeping Flora entertained, that she should be examining the suicidal motivations of American poets, several of whom such as Anne Sexton and Sylvia Plath, were mothers with daughters as well.

3. Gill, Jelena Bulat. "Nobody Under the Rose." Birch Lane Presents American Fiction: The Best Unpublished Short Stories by Emerging Writers. Eds. Michael C. White and Alan Davis. New York: Carol Publishing Group, 1990. 137 – 156.

The daughter in this story, more of a domestic slave to her mother than a daughter, grows up vulnerable to disguised acts of kindness and unable to express her own feelings because she has been physically and emotionally neglected by her only parent. When Thelma's father dies, her mother grumbles at the grave: " 'For all the years I've known him, there was nothing he wouldn't do to make me feel miserable' " (137). It is to five-year-old Thelma that she turns next to become her designated scapegoat, the source of her self-inflicted misery. Left alone by her mother for long periods of time as a child, Thelma grows up deprived of both a maternal role model as well as friendships and many of the happy experiences of childhood. As an adult, Thelma resorts to prostitution and allows herself to be abused by those who sense an emotional vulnerability in her character and prey upon it. Long after her mother has died, Thelma remains a solitary hermit, a neglected oddity of society who was never given the maternal nurturing and emotional support she needed during childhood to adjust to the world beyond her mother's door.

4. Hempel, Amy. "Tom-Rock Through the Eels." At the Gates of the Animal Kingdom. New York: Alfred A. Knopf, 1990. 119 – 127.

In the wake of her mother's suicide, the daughter-protagonist of this story responds to her grandmother's plea to "help me remember the good times with your mother" because anti-depressants have robbed her aging mind of details (122). While the daughter sleeps in the bed where her mother's body was discovered and sifts through childhood recollections, she can recall few "good times" to share with her grandmother. "Every so often we tried to shop together," she remembers, "tried to bake together, tried together to teach ourselves something from a how-to book. Mostly I did things around her, the way nurses change the sheets with the patient still in bed" (123).

The special mother-daughter memories she does recall from the past are those of friends' mothers—the mother who let her daughter keep her underwear in a fondue pot sprayed with Estee Lauder or the mother who still threw her arm across the passenger seat to protect her teenage daughter when the car had to stop quickly—but not her own. "My mother wore me like a fur," she recalls, but never attempted to develop a close relationship with her daughter.

5. Jamal, Sauda. "A Mother That Loves You." Lesbian Fiction: An Anthology. Ed. Elly Bulkin. Watertown: Persephone Press, 1981. 239 – 244.

The legacy the black mother in this narrative passes on to her adolescent daughter is one of drug addiction and theft to support their mutual habit. When Bones is caught shoplifting a coat, the security guard does not press charges but mercifully allows her to go free. " 'I mean, somewhere you have a mother that loves you, it shows,' " he tells Bones. " 'You got no business getting yourself into a jam like this' " (240). But Bones knows if she had given the guard her real address in the slum neighborhood, he would have likely sent her straight to jail. For she returns to a home that offers only occasional heat and a mother who congratulates her on to ability to steal so well at the young age of 14. " 'You's a real hustler,' " she says as she hugs her daughter, " 'won't have my baby busin' huh ass from nine ta five or whorin' for no man. You can make money on your own, a real hustler . . . ' " (243 – 244). As mother and daughter inject heroin into their veins, Bones tries to convince herself that the policeman was right: she does have a mother who loves her because unlike other daughters of the neighborhood, at least she has yet to be abandoned.

6. Moody, Anne. "The Cow." Mr. Death: Four Stories. New York: Harper and Row, 1975. 25 – 49.

The poor, black mother in this narrative comes to despise her own daughter as yet another symbol of her own unfortunate fate in life. When Truelove and her husband marry, her mother-in-law offers the couple a pregnant cow as a wedding present. Truelove views the gift "as a testament of her mother-in-law's feelings toward her," for instead of offering a docile, mild-mannered animal, she gives her her also-pregnant daughter-in-law "the most mischievous, discontented, humanlike, rebellious cow this side of China" (27 – 28). As Truelove's daughter grows, her mother sees disturbing resemblances between Louella and the cow. "Same as the cow was always doing things to annoy and embarrass Truelove, the older Louella got the more she began to do the same" (42). Truelove even notices her daughter beginning to physically resemble the cow with her bulging eyes and frequently cocked head. As Louella grows older, so annoying and spiteful is she to her mother that Truelove begins to abuse her daughter, "but the more Truelove beat Louella the more stubborn the child got" (45). Louella has no friends and cannot socialize with other children without conflict. Like the cow, she is confined to the farm. And so it is that when True love discovers she is pregnant again and her husband is having an affair, she spends most of her day rocking on the front porch, "thinking about her life and wondering whether it was fate or just her stupidity that had landed her there in that bottom of sand" (47). In this dejected state of mind, Truelove accepts without any sign of emotion the sudden death of her daughter beneath the wheels of a young driver who swerves his automobile to miss the cow crossing the road but crushes Louella, chasing behind. The death of her daughter seems but one more strike against an already numbed Truelove whose life has become mired in misery.

7. Neville, Susan. "The Invention of Flight." The Invention of Flight. Athens: University of Georgia Press, 1984. 92 – 109.

The mother-daughter relationship in this narrative is observed from the viewpoint of the psychologist-landlord who narrates the story. Living in the same house with the mother and daughter, she witnesses and deplores the obvious neglect and lack of love in their relationship which has left the daughter a socially withdrawn, dependent 35-year-old virgin with little confidence and few aspirations. The narrator characterizes the mother as a self-centered woman, so obviously intent upon her own pursuit of pleasure that there is no room in her life to consider her daughter's happiness as well. The narrator laments:

> The mother is so happy and the daughter in such obvious misery that I am convinced the mother has in some way made Melissa the way that she is, that it is she who is completely responsible for what Melissa has become, as if she gave birth to her to absorb her spirit; I am certain there is no love between them. (95)

The emotional devastation that can result from a mother's neglect of her daughter's needs is clearly illustrated in Neville's story.

8. Nugent, Beth. "Another Country." City of Boys. New York: Alfred A. Knopf, 1992. 96 – 127.

The adolescent daughter in this story is rejected by her natural father, who begins a new family of his own following his divorce from the narrator's mother, and neglected by her alcoholic mother who attempts to find acceptance of her own through a series of short-time lovers she always introduces individually to her daughter as "your Uncle." Forced to live in a cold and dreary apartment building in a poor section of New York City, the narrator feels trapped by the circumstances of her life and maternal neglect she cannot change. She writes:

> Right now my father is sitting down to dinner, smiling absently at the bright blond heads of his new children while my brother sits in a dark room, turning to stone. In the alley, pigeons rise and settle anxiously, shaking off the growing chill. Mother, I want to call out, Mother, I am dying, but she is falling once again into the arms of a man she loves. (127)

9. Oates, Joyce Carol. "The Children." Motherlove: Stories by Women about Motherhood. Ed. Stephanie Spinner. New York: Dell, 1978. 160 – 182.

The young mother in this story becomes abusive as the result of her obsession with first time motherhood, to the exclusion of all other aspects of her life. Ginny's perception of reality becomes so limited and distorted by the confines of motherhood that she eventually erupts in a violent rage of displaced anger at her young daughter. When she gives up her career with the birth of Rachel, Ginny immerses herself in the daily demands and pleasures of mothering, sacrificing other interests she might have pursued to keep her perspective in balance. With the company of other mothers in her suburban neighborhood as her only social outlet, Ginny gradually begins to realize and resent the fact that she has lost touch with the woman she once was prior to marriage and childbirth, that her identity has become confused with that of her two children.

She summoned up intelligently the differences that lay between her and the woman she had become, this rather slovenly mother with nondescript hair and a fretful, maternal frown, a husband who never quite looked at her and did not need to look at her. Yes, there was a difference. It seemed to her that everyone else moved without defenses and without disguise, while she was never quite herself, always harassed or taken off guard. (173)

When Rachel's younger brother is born, Ginny mistakenly interprets Rachel's jealousy of him and her actions to gain equal attention as potentially violent and harmful, as if "some demented force of disorder and brutality" is driving her daughter. Overexaggerating the natural sibling rivalry manifest in her daughter's behavior, Ginny develops a paranoid view of her daughter as a potential threat to her infant's life who must be stopped, even if she must resort to violence to protect her son from harm. Oates's frightening portrayal defines a woman narrowed by the experience of motherhood. This young mother's perceptions become so demented by the restrictive confines of her world that she lashes out violently at her young daughter who becomes the abused scapegoat of her own maternal frustration.

10. Oates, Joyce Carol. "The Madwoman." The Seduction and Other Stories. Los Angeles: Black Sparrow Press, 1975. 202 – 209.

In desperation, the adolescent daughter in this story seeks help from strangers on the street to escape her abusive mother. An alcoholic, her mother lives in filth and self-deprecation, raising her daughter in an environment of neglect and squalor. She has threatened to burn the house down more than once, her daughter confides in the man and woman from whom she seeks assistance and protection. But the mother denies her daughter's accusations and refuses help for her condition, calling her daughter a "little bitch of a liar" with a tremendous imagination.

11. Patai, Daphne. "On Your Fifty-fifth Birthday." Aphra. 5.3 (1974): 65 – 72.

This story examines the feelings of an adult daughter, expressed directly to her estranged mother, who abandoned her two daughters to be raised by surrogate parents when they were only four and five years old when she realized she was unable to accept the responsibilities of motherhood. When mother and the daughter-narrator are reunited several years later, they move between "affection and estrangement, perhaps suffering from both at once." The mother demands explanations for her daughter's silences, while she is quick to remind her mother: "I claimed the same right as you to aloneness" (70). The narrator feels a continuing bitterness toward her mother, despite their efforts to build a closer relationship. "I watched you and my old, old hurt increased," the narrator silently acknowledges her feelings to herself shortly before her mother leaves. "My feelings were just and unjust—always the two—and this knowledge increased the pain. Could we not comfort one another?" (71). As mother and daughter part, the daughter realizes that despite her mother's efforts to nurture a bond with her daughter, in many respects she will always remain a mysterious stranger who may realize now that she loves her daughters, but cannot let them into her life.

12. Roberts, Nancy. "The Bruise." Women and Other Bodies of Water. Port Townsend, WA: Dragon Gate, Inc., 1987. 15 – 24.

    The mother in this narrative refuses to acknowledge that her daughter is a victim of incestuous sexual abuse. Although the adult narrator tries to confide the truth to her mother, her mother averts her daughter's attempted confession even as she defends her husband's innocence. While she accepts her daughter's refusal to move back home, even though living in New York City is clearly dangerous for her as a single woman, this mother denies the primary reason that keeps her daughter living at a safe distance from her father's potential abuse.

13. Shaid, Fatima. "Before Echo." The Mayor of New Orleans: Just Talking Jazz. Berkeley: Creative Arts Book Company, 1987. 89 – 143.

    The mother in this story attempts to make up for the abandonment and neglect of her daughter after she is reunited with her for the first time after many years. During her adolescence Joan learns that the woman who abandoned her at birth could not bear the solitude of living in the swamp, where Joan has spent most of her life, and preferred the excitement of the city. Since she was 17 years old, her mother has earned her living as a prostitute in the French Quarter of New Orleans and never attempted to contact her daughter. " 'Didn't you want a daughter?' " Joan questions her mother when they finally meet in New Orleans. " 'I wanted you to be better than me,' " her mother explains her distance of so many years (140). As Oceola candidly describes her life of illegally selling her body, a product that has cheapened with age, and the other crimes which invariably accompany prostitution, Joan tries to patiently understand this woman who is her mother. But Oceola has been "out in the street so long she could not imagine the mentality of a virgin" and talks to Joan as if she were another woman of the streets. When she describes her unwanted daughter as a "thing" she once discarded, Joan leaves, convinced "she has seen the reality of her mother and could give her up" (141 – 142). But when she returns to the swamp, Joan discovers her mother waiting there, prepared to accept her daughter's advice to rebuild her life differently and experience motherhood for the first time.

14. Slosberg, Deborah. "Desert Landscapes." Calyx. 3.1 (1990/91): 68 – 79.

    The daughter of an alcoholic mother narrates this innovative narrative of maternal neglect. The series of vignettes which comprise the narrative describe the self-absorbed outlook of the mother and her relationship—or lack of a relationship—with her daughter. "I laugh because," the narrator writes, "so drunk, she crosses three streets to the mailbox in her black brassiere & panties. I laugh when, returning, she trips on the stair, when the Chianti she carries shatters green feather-thin scraps of glass across grey cement, purple wine. I laugh because I know then I will never be like her, she is the end of the line" (69). The daughter grows up unsure that anyone really loves her and emotionally vulnerable to the possibility of love, for she has been deprived of the most of all assurances maternal love.

15. Thomas, Audrey. "Real Mothers." Real Mothers: Short Stories by Audrey Thomas. Vancouver: Talonbooks, 1981. 9 – 22.

The daughters in this story experience maternal neglect when their recently divorced mother begins living with a lover and gradually distances herself from them. The divorce confuses the daughters at first, who never observed harsh words to pass between their parents. Only Marie-Anne heard her mother's weeping upstairs in the middle of the night. "She wanted to go up and comfort her mother, but didn't know what to say. She lay awake and tried to understand about her father having to leave" (9). The daughters share their mother's happiness over her weight loss and decision to return to school following the divorce. But when her first lover following the divorce moves in, they feel their mother becoming more and more distant emotionally. The daughters know their estrangement has become complete one night when their mother announces they have been too close as a family and must learn to "be a little more separate." She ends the conversation by requesting her children to call her by her first name, Helen. It is when Helen's lover turns his affectionate advances toward the daughters as well that they conclude they can no longer live with their mother. As they drive away with their father one snowy morning to begin living with him and his new wife, all too late Helen realizes her neglect of her daughters and futilely chases after the car in her nightgown screaming, " 'Don't take my baby from me, don't take my baby from me, don't take. . . .' " (22).

16. Tinsley, Molly Best. "Zoe." Homeplaces: Stories of the South by Women Writers. Ed. Mary Ellis Gibson. Columbia: University of South Carolina Press, 1991. 196 – 211.

This story examines an emotionally neglected, bulimic daughter's longing for stability in her adolescent life which her sensual, free-spirited mother, too preoccupied with her stream of one-night lovers to develop a close mother-daughter relationship, cannot offer. In one longer-term lover Zoe discovers the stability and caring her mother has never been able to provide and recognizes someone she can both love and admire.

17. Williams, Joy. "Escapes." Escapes. New York: Atlantic Monthly Press, 1990. 1 – 14.

A daughter recalling her childhood in this narrative remembers her mother's alcoholism as a painful and embarrassing addiction she was never able to overcome. Her mother, she remembers, always "smelled then like the glass that was always in the sink in the morning, and the smell reminds me still of daring and deception, hopes and little lies" (6). Although the narrator's mother and she were always "linked in our hopeless and uncomprehending love of one another," they were never able to form a close relationship because of the alcoholism barrier that divided them and eventually caused the mother's death (4).

2

Aging

INTRODUCTION

As mothers age, the mother-daughter relationship inevitably changes, the stories in this chapter illustrate. A reversal of roles often occurs, with adult daughters assuming traditional maternal responsibilities as their mothers become less able to care for themselves. Adult daughters both sympathize and identify with their mothers' fate as they age. In the worn faces and wrinkled bodies of their mothers, these daughters see a reflection of themselves to come as they too grow older. Yet these frail and often helpless mothers still often wield an incredible amount of power over the lives of their daughters, as evidenced in this mother-daughter literature.

Short fictions written by Paulette Bates Alden, Joyce Reiser Kornblatt, Cordinne Demas Bliss, and Florence Chanock Cohen explore the issue of daughters caring for their aging mothers, a process which can bond mothers and daughters closer together or further alienate the two in bitter frustration. In the story "Legacies" a grandmother, mother, and granddaughter all become entangled in the issue of the grandmother's care. Paulette Bates Alden's narrative poses difficult questions: Are daughters obligated to care for their aging mothers? What happens when mother and daughter cannot agree on the kind of care that best meets the mother's needs and cannot communicate without argument and friction? A similar conflict develops in Joyce Reiser Kornblatt's "Ordinary Mysteries" when an aging mother recuperating from a seizure and her daughter cannot resolve the issue of care. Although the mother realizes her helplessness has burdened her daughter ("As if she has been kidnapped, this illness of mine has ripped her out of her world and tied her to my sudden helplessness," she admits), she refuses to acknowledge that she can no longer live by herself (195). This mother's inability to accept her limitations and her stubborn independence leave her daughter with difficult choices for her future care. The mother in Corinne Demas Bliss's "Small Sins" also refuses nursing home care in favor of living in her daughter's home, yet her petulance and constant demands annoy her daughter so much that she finally admits to her face that she does not love her anymore. The daughter in Florence Chanock Cohen's "The Golden Triangle" faces equally unpleasant alternatives for the care of her aging mother when the administrator of a hotel for the elderly determines that her mother is not sane enough to be accepted as a resident. Freya is left with two equally undesirable options of either admitting her mother to a nursing home or continuing to care for her mother at home, which her husband has all but forbidden. A husband's refusal to allow his mother-in-law to live with her daughter in Edith Konecky's "Turn Your Back and Walk Away" leaves his wife with no other alternative but to leave her mother in a nursing home, where she sees signs of deterioration in her mother's condition with each depressing visit. Her lack of choice does not diminish the feelings of guilt and anguish which resurface each time she must leave her mother in a place filled with so much loneliness.

If the care of an aging mother can be a burden for an adult daughter, the experience can also provide the opportunity for continued bonding between mothers and daughters, as stories written by Mary Jane Moffat and Annette Sanford illustrate. The daughter in Moffat's "Giving My Mother a Bath" very carefully and lovingly bathes the fragile, wrinkled body of her mother with great care, as she remembers her childhood when she was the one bathed by her mother—a very feminine woman who always "smelled of Blue Grass, not the faint, dank vapors of age. She was never sick," the narrator recalls. "And she was never, ever going to die" (101). Now she cannot escape the fact that her mother will eventually die, and the bathing routine becomes a special bonding ritual for mother and daughter. Similarly, the adult daughter in Sanford's "Standing By" offers her aging mother constant emotional and physical support as she undergoes dental surgery. But watching her mother resting peacefully after the operation only serves to remind the daughter that the aging process will eventually sever forever the special bond which unites them.

Daughters such as those portrayed in Ilona Karmel's "Fru Holm" and Mary Ward Brown's "It Wasn't All Dancing" are rare in this century's American fiction. Even daughters who have been mistreated or abandoned by their mothers earlier during their lives usually remain faithful to their aging mothers. The daughter's callous treatment of her mother and indifference to her feelings in Karmel's narrative and the daughter's avoidance of her aging mother in Brown's story are uncharacteristic of most adult daughters in these stories who patiently and compassionately care for their aging mothers, despite their frequent senility, irritability, and helplessness.

Even if their bodies and minds are failing them as they age, mothers are still able to exert much power over their daughters, these writings indicate. The aging mothers in Corinne Demas Bliss's "Small Sins" and Estelle Bamberg's "A Portrait of Mama" still attempt to direct their daughters' behavior and manipulate their lives, even though they are adult women. The daughter in "Small Sins" vows never to force her aging mother to leave her home, even though her presence is often unbearable, because she would feel too much guilt abandoning her mother. "I don't want her to ever have that kind of power over me," she tells her brother while she obviously fails to recognize the control her mother already exerts over her life (55). The aging but crafty mother in "A Portrait of Mama" schemes and manipulates circumstances until her powerless daughter is left with no other alternative but to invite her to come live with her family.

The authors of these stories provide insight into how the aging process affects the minds of women. While the mother in Jonis Agee's "Each Time We Meet" borders on insanity and renounces her two daughters, the 92-year-old mother in Audrey Thomas's "Sunday Morning, June 4, 1989" becomes so preoccupied with herself that she is unaware that traumatic world events are changing history while she worries about being evicted from her apartment. While the middle-aged mother in Sandra Thompson's

"Ashes" withdraws from social contact and gradually wills herself to die, the aging mother in Maxine Kumin's "West" maintains self-reliance on a rural farm and seeks alternatives to motherhood now that her daughters are grown so that she can continue her own lifelong quest for self-actualization. When the mother in Lisa Koger's "Structural Changes" realizes she no longer controls the direction of her adult daughter's life, she retreats into a dream world where she is safely in command.

Their mothers' loss of will to live concerns adult daughters in several of these stories. Daughters in Anne Hemenway's "A Good Life" and Sandra Thompson's "Ashes" try in vain to revitalize their mothers' interest in living. The tall and beautiful mother whom the adult daughter in "Ashes" remembers from childhood has been replaced by a dark and thin woman with half-closed eyes who hibernates from the world, chain smoking and drinking alcohol all day. Even the thought of a visit to the beauty parlor, at the suggestion of her daughter, is too intimidating for this reclusive mother to face. The daughter in "A Good Life" mourns the wasted potential she knows is trapped inside her mother, whose life has disintegrated into television and alcohol addiction. The mother refuses to change while she insists that she is content with her life as it is.

Unresolved conflicts inevitably surface as mothers and daughters age. But reconciliation of these conflicts may still be possible, the writers of these fictions suggest. The protagonists of Mary Morris's "Death Apples" become more like sisters than mother and daughter when a Caribbean vacation promises an opportunity for emotional healing and adventure. The mother and daughter in Joanna Higgins's "Dancing at the Holland" grow closer when the aging mother confesses the source of alienation which has stood between them for so many years.

But stories authored by Mae Briskin and R. M. Kinder remind us that building a closer mother-daughter relationship may be impossible for aging mothers whose martyrdom and inability to forgive their daughters, as demonstrated in Briskin's "Present Tense," and whose own self-centeredness, as illustrated in Kinder's "Cora's Room," stand in the way of reconciliation. As the mother and daughter in "Present Tense" reach an impasse in their inability to communicate, the daughter finally realizes that neither reconciliation nor complete severance is possible in their relationship. "We are past explanation or apology," she admits. "We are separate at last, and we are inseparable after all" (166).

Aging mothers pass on a cultural heritage of mixed value to their daughters in these short fictions. The two daughters in Susan Nunes's "A Moving Day" inherit an uncertain wealth of memory and culture when their aging mother begins to shed her possessions as she prepares to move to a home for the aged. The daughters search in vain for the messages that they know must lie behind each of these objects but fear have been lost in the process of "growing up and growing old." "We open drawers, peer into the recesses of cupboards, rummage through the depths of closets," explains one of the daughters. "What a lot of stuff! We lift, untuck, unwrap, and set aside. The message is there, we know. But what is it? Perhaps if we knew, then we wouldn't have to puzzle out our mother's righteous determination to shed the past" (131). The Jewish daughter in Francine Krasno's "Celia," disappointed in what she perceives as the failure of her mother's life, seeks stories of her grandmother and greatgrandmother in hopes of discovering a link with her past that she can admire. "I want to know what they have done so I will know what is possible for myself," she writes (245). "My greatest fear has been that I would grow to be like my mother: passive, discontented, confined. I want to know if there has been a time in her life when she was not all of these things. I want to find something to like in her. Which will be something to like in myself. Perhaps in my maternal history there is one story that is my own" (246). In contrast, the adult daughter in Kim Chernin's "The "Proposal" seeks to preserve a dying shtelt culture as well as the memory of her aging, immigrant mother when she agrees to write her mother's recollections. As the daughter begins listening to her mother's life story, an image forms in her mind in which she sees herself as symbolic of many women entrusted with the responsibility of keeping alive the memories of their mothers and passing these remembrances on to their daughters. She describes her vision:

> An image comes to me. I see generations of women bearing a flame. It is hidden, buried deep within, yet there are handing it down from one to another, burning. It is a gift of fire, transported from a world far off and far away, but never extinguished. And now, in this very moment, my mother imparts the care of it to me. I must keep it alive, I must manage not to be consumed by it, I must hand it on when the time comes to my daughter. (80 – 81).

SHORT FICTION

18. Agee, Jonis. "Each Time We Meet." Bend This Heart. St. Paul: Coffee House Press, 1989. 61 – 65.

    Insanity threatens the aging mother in this story, alienating her husband and daughters who commit her to a nearby mental hospital. The mother neither welcomes her daughters' visit nor expresses any desire to see them again once they reach the hospital. " 'This is goodbye,' " she announces to her daughters. " 'I never want to see you again' " (65). Consoling their father, who has been accused of murder by their mother, the daughters in the story commit to long-term psychiatric care a woman who can no longer function as a mother, a woman who has entered a world of delusion and paranoia from which she may never escape.

19. Alden, Paulette Bates. "Legacies." Feeding the Eagles. St. Paul: Graywolf Press, 1988. 15 – 34.

    The relationship of three generations of mothers and daughters is examined in this narrative. As the grandmother in the story enters the final phase of her life, her care becomes an issue of conflict the three women must resolve. Their dilemma raises several questions which confront aging mothers and their adult daughters: Who is responsible to decide the best alternative when an aging mother can no longer care for herself or make rational decisions concerning her care? Are daughters obligated to care for their aging mothers? What happens when the aging mother and her daughter disagree on the mother's future care and cannot communicate without anger and hurt feelings? And, in this particular story, where does this awkward situation leave the granddaughter of the family who wants to maintain a relationship with both her mother and grandmother but is caught between the two women and their inability to reconcile their conflicting viewpoints? These are the questions Alden explores in this story of the aging process and its effect upon mothers and daughters.

20. Bamberg, Estelle. "A Portrait of Mama." Prize College Stories, 1963. Ed. Whit and Hallie Burnett. New York: Random House, 1963. 91 – 102.

This characterization of an aging mother, written from her daughter's perspective, emphasizes the control that mothers wield over their daughters, even into adulthood. With deliberate intention and rather impressive strategy, the aging mother in this story manipulates circumstances until her daughter is left with no alternative but to invite her widowed mother to come and live with her family. The daughter writes that she has given up trying to reason with her mother. "It's like trying to scream under water," she admits (94). Conflicting emotions for her mother of exasperation and compassion grip the daughter as she finally gives in and bids her mother's wish, recognizing with foreboding that wherever her mother has lived "the walls seem to tumble down in anger and despair" (102).

21. Barnhill, Susan. "Near Places, Far Places." When I Am An Old Woman I Shall Wear Purple: An Anthology of Short Stories and Poetry. Ed. Sandra Martz. Manhattan Beach, CA: Papier-Mache Press, 1987. 23 – 37.

A widowed adult daughter grows more content living with her aging mother in this story when she begins to place the emotional needs of her mother above her own self-centered motives. At first the narrator urges her mother to sell the last of her treasured handmade quilts because, she realizes in retrospect, "those quilts would go places I'd never been and see sights I'd never seen, and probably never would. There I was," the daughter-narrator admits, "not able to admit to a soul that a bunch of patchwork quilts made by my grannie and great-aunts and women so long since dead I couldn't recall their names, that a bunch of old quilts had made me but one thing and that was jealous" (28). Just as the sales transaction is about to take place, the daughter intercedes, allowing her mother the joy of saving her last and most prized quilt. A wave of contentment replaces the daughter's feelings of jealousy as she sits with her mother, rocking peacefully on the front porch of their North Carolina home, just "a couple of old women looking out at the darkness and listening to the summer sounds, and grateful for a big old house with a good view" (37).

22. Bliss, Corinne Demas. "Small Sins." What We Save for Last. Minneapolis: Milkweed Editions, 1992. 49 – 55.

The often unacknowledged power that aging mothers exert over their daughters is illustrated in this story. Even though the adult daughter depicted by Bliss is bold enough to admit to her mother directly that does not love her anymore and openly resents the intrusion of her mother (who refuses to live in a nursing home) in her home, she has promised herself that she will tolerate her mother's presence until her death. " 'You know, I'm sure,' " she writes to her brother, " 'I'm doing it for myself, not for her. (In one of our more awful scenes, just now in fact, she bullied me into admitting I didn't love her.) It's not masochism at all. It's that I don't want to ever have anything to feel guilty about. I don't want her to ever have that kind of power over me' " (55).

23. Briskin, Mae. "Present Tense." A Boy Like Astrid's Mother. New York: W. W. Norton, 1988. 154 – 166.

"My mother searches for misery and, when she finds it, accuses me of bringing it," begins the adult daughter who narrates this story, irrevocably estranged from her aging mother who harbors repressed anger at her inability to control her daughter's life, much less her own (154). A begrudging martyr, the mother thrives on attempts to manipulate her daughter with guilt and refusal to forgive. With practice, the daughter has analyzed these maternal mind games and refuses to be cornered by her mother's self-serving strategies. The daughter finds it hard to believe that her aging mother continues her role as a subservient wife to an indifferent husband. From years of conditioning her mother serves her husband meals faithfully while she eats only bread as she stands at the kitchen sink washing dishes, a practice only mothers can understand, she once told her daughter. Before her mother dies, the narrator writes, "I want her to discover she is her husband's equal" (157). Even though she is anemic and almost blind from neglect of herself, the mother refuses any help for herself, hissing defiantly at her daughter, " 'I don't *need* you' " (165). The daughter's self-control and tolerance finally give way to rage against her mother's stubborn independence and accusatory judgments. The two stand rigidly confronting one another, as the narrator concludes: "We are silent. Nor could we move toward one another if we were commanded to. We are past explanation or apology. We are separate at last, and we are inseparable after all" (166).

24. Brodine, Karen. "Here, Take My Words." When I Am An Old Woman I Shall Wear Purple: An Anthology of Short Stories and Poetry. Ed. Sandra Martz. Manhattan Beach, CA: Papier-Mache Press, 1987. 14 – 17.

Three generations of mothers and daughters in this narrative mourn the grandmother's increasing senility and inability to care for herself. An hour's visit to the grandmother's nursing home "seems like a long time," the daughter-narrator writes. Mother and daughter leave "because we can't bear to stay any longer" (17). The woman who was once the "strongest person" her granddaughter knew now lies strapped to her bed, yearning for the past as a distant "wished-for land" where she remembers being in control of her life. Despite her deteriorating mental condition, the grandmother realizes she is a captive of the present who has become increasingly dependent upon others while she has little control of her own life left.

25. Chernin, Kim. "The Proposal." My Mother's Daughter: Stories by Women. Ed. Irene Zahava. Freedom, CA: The Crossing Press, 1991. 65 – 82.

An adult daughter begins writing the life of her aging immigrant mother in this story as she seeks to preserve the memory not only of a longtime Community revolutionary but her mother's recollections of the Old World shtelt culture as well, which will undoubtedly perish with the passing of her generation. The narrator's mother arrived in America at the age of 12 and supported her family members when her father ran away and deserted them. "To me," the daughter writes, "she gave everything she must have wanted for herself, a girl of thirteen or fourteen, walking home from the factory, exhausted after a day of work" (79). As a child, the narrator remembers challenging her mother's opinions and ideals. "Any opinion she uttered," the daughter writes, "I took the opposite point of view. If she liked realism, I preferred abstract art. If she believed in internationalism, I spoke about the necessity to concentrate on local conditions" (70). And now, years later, the daughter confesses: "I am torn by contradiction. I love this woman. She was my first great aching love. All my life I have wanted to do whatever she asked of me, in spite of our quarreling" (76). What her mother now asks of her daughter is that she record the events of her extraordinary life. To undertake this project will mean that the daughter must put aside her own poetry writing, which her mother dismisses lightly as lacking in social value. "She's old, I say to myself," writes the narrator. "She's never asked anything from you as a writer before. Give this. You can always go back to your own work later" (76). As the mother begins to relate the circumstances of her life, an image forms in the mind of the daughter-narrator that gives validity and a sense of purpose to her undertaking. She describes the vision:

> An image comes to me. I see generations of women bearing a flame. It is hidden, buried deep within, yet they are handing it down from one to another, burning. It is a gift of fire, transported from a world far off and far away, but never extinguished. And now, in this very moment, my mother imparts the care of it to me. I must keep it alive, I must manage not to be consumed by it, I must hand it on when the time comes to my daughter. (80 – 81)

26. Cohen, Florence Chanock. "The Golden Triangle." The Monkey Puzzle Tree. Chicago: Story Press, 1979. 87 – 100.

The middle-aged daughter in this story tries in vain to move her aging mother from her home to a selective hotel for the elderly. The hotel administrator who interviews Mrs. Gould rejects her as a possible resident on the basis of her "inappropriate responses," explaining to her daughter that "a place for the old and a place for the senile are two different things. . ." (99). Mrs. Gould suffers from lapses of memory and a refusal to accept the death of her first daughter. A nursing home would be a more appropriate residence, the hotel administrator advises. Her decision leaves Freya with two equally unpleasant alternatives. She can commit her mother to a nursing home or allow her to return to her own home, a decision which she knows her husband will not approve. In a reversal of roles the daughter of this story assumes the role of a mother who must accept the responsibility to determine the future care of her childlike mother while she also faces the frightening realization that she can no longer be assured of her mother's sanity.

27. Hampl, Patricia. "Look at a Teacup." The Best American Short Stories 1977. Ed. Martha Foley. Boston: Houghton Mifflin, 1977. 181 – 187.

The daughter of a woman married at the beginning of World War Two tries to piece together her mother's personal history as she attempts to place it in context of world history at the same time in this narrative. Reluctant to uncover her past, which she deems as inconsequential in the scheme of history, the narrator's mother advises her daughter not to dwell in the past, but look toward the future. " 'Look ahead,' " she tells her. " 'Life goes on, you can't keep going over things. It's the *flow* of life that counts' " (185). The narrator tries to follow her mother's advice but cannot ignore the significance of the past. She writes:

> I try, but everything drives me into the past that she insists is safely gone. How can I ride forward on her errand when all the world, even the smallest object, sends me back, sets me wondering over and over about our own strange life and country, always trying to understand history and sexuality. Details, however small, get sorted into their appropriate stories, all right, but I am always holding out for the past and thinking how it keeps coming back at us. (185)

Exploring the details of her mother's past and the historical events of her lifetime helps this daughter understand her own identity and heritage.

28. Hayden, Julie. "Eighteen Down." The Lists of the Past. New York: Viking Press, 1976. 95 – 101.

The adult daughter in this story tries to inject new life into her aging mother as they await news of the outcome of her father's operation. The daughter's attempts to divert her mother's attention from the anxiety of waiting and alter her lifestyle in a healthier direction are met with an obstinate resistance to change on her mother's part, who is stubbornly comfortable with her established routine of crossword puzzles, cigarette smoke, drawn curtains, and little exercise. It is the daughter in this story who realizes she is powerless to change her mother's behavior and must accept her as she is.

29. Hemenway, Anne. "A Good Life." Intro 9: Close to Home. Eds. George Garrett and Michael Mewshaw. Austin: Hendel and Reinke, 1978. 83 – 91.

This narrative characterizes a middle-aged mother whose life has disintegrated into television and alcohol addiction and reflects the frustrations of her daughter who sees wasted potential trapped inside her mother's deteriorating body. "It is hard to see the spirit and daring in my mother," the narrator begins her story, as she proceeds to describe her mother as a "self-contained" woman, in and out of mental hospitals with bizarre fantasies, who isolates herself from close relationships and keeps almost constant company with gin and tonic. "Her need for absolute privacy overrides the loneliness she sometimes feels," writes the narrator. Yet, her fear of abandonment makes her cling to her only daughter for companionship. At the insistence of her daughter that she change her life, the mother counters, " 'I like my life the way it is. I don't want to change. I don't want to fight' " (91). Her life, the mother convinces herself, has been better and more exciting that most. Her devoted daughter, she insists is "living proof" of the quality of the life she has led. She has earned a rest. " 'It's a good life,' " she proclaims (91).

30. Higgins, Joanna. "Dancing at the Holland." Birch Lane Press Presents American Fiction: The Best Unpublished Short Stories by Emerging Writers. Eds. Michael C. White and Alan Davis. New York: Carol Publishing Group, 1990. 170 – 184.

An aging mother and her daughter grow closer in this story as the mother resolves to live despite her approaching blindness and her daughter begins to understand the cause of her mother's past alienation. During their lengthy drive to an opthomologist's clinic where each hopes for a miracle cure, the conversation of the narrator's 81-year-old mother is dominated with thoughts of her already preplanned cremation and funeral service. In the purse of the narrator lies the reminder she has written to herself, "*Just Say Yes*," for she knows that to argue with her mother about her death at this point would only heighten her mother's "volatile blood pressure" and rekindle their "history of argument, ineradicable differences" (172). "What if I go first, then what?" the narrator ponders as they cross the sugar beet fields of the upper Midwest. Aging mothers, even blinding, aging mothers, do not always precede their children in death. "Compared to everything else, death is easy," she realizes (173). When the costly medical visit produces no hope for a cure for her mother's condition, the narrator feels intense guilt for promoting the visit, putting her mother through the additional stress of the trip, plus the disappointment of the outcome. But her mother seems resigned to her prognosis, relieved that the uncertainty is over, comfortable with her future. The daughter hears hope in her mother's voice during the long drive home. "A variation, inversion of the theme. I hear it in her voice, and the fragile resolve there. It touches me," she writes (183). As mother and daughter talk, the mother confesses that long ago she almost killed her young daughter during one of the most unhappy periods of her marriage, a revelation which helps to explain the distance that has separated them all of these years. The narrator writes:

> All these years. What words of mind to reach that depth? Relieve the press of emotion. Hers. Mine. Her words parting curtains upon curtains of loss. Guilt. That distance between us all this time, the withholding, the way the air used to go storm-still around her, the way she would hide out in their bedroom at the top of the house, crying, alone, up there. Trying to get away from us—the storm lasting, sometimes, several days. The exile. (182 – 183)

Absorbing their past and anticipating the future, mother and daughter feel a newfound sense of closeness during their drive home as they plan together for the changes ahead in their lives.

31. Howland, Bette. "How We Got the Old Woman to Go." Blue in Chicago. New York: Harper and Row, 1978. 149 – 183.

The occasion of a grandmother's funeral provides an opportunity for the mothers and daughters of the family in this story to reevaluate their attitudes toward motherhood. While the aging mothers grew up during the postwar era when women did not question motherhood, the daughters have been reared during an era of choice and alternatives, many choosing not to become mothers themselves. Accused of not giving their mothers grandchildren, the daughters defend their decision with the weapon of silence. "What better way to tell your mother what you think of her than not to have children? That was what they had to say for themselves. Their silence was accusing" (179). What started out as hostility between these generations of women evolves into a revelation for the mothers who begin to realize they never wanted children, "should never have had Daughters in the first place. No wonder it had all been so difficult. They had been bilked, conned, hoodwinked, swindled, sold a bill of goods" (181). Their daughters now want "just what the Mothers wanted out of life. Only they wanted more. And they wanted it now. And they knew how to get it. They weren't going to run the race for happiness in any three-legged sack" (181). For the aging mothers of this family it is too late to begin life again. They can only envy their new breed of daughters, now approaching middle age themselves, who have grown up more independent and convinced that motherhood is not a necessity for their fulfillment as women.

32. Karmel, Ilona. "Fru Holm." 40 Best Stories from Mademoiselle 1935 – 1960. Eds. Cyrilly Abels and Margarita G. Smith. New York: Harper and Brothers, 1960. 393 – 411.

A daughter attempts to gradually sever her relationship with her aging mother when she admits her to a nursing home in this story. Surrounded by dying women, Fru Holm is obviously out of place with her good health. Realizing that she does not belong, Fru Holm withdraws socially from the other nursing home residents. Despite her pleas to her daughter to allow her to leave, the mother's wishes are dismissed by her daughter as foolish and unreasonable. As her daughter continues to distance herself from her mother with only occasional, perfunctory visits to the home, Fru Holm dies at the age of 72, not of physical causes but from loneliness and rejection by her indifferent daughter.

33. Kinder, R. M. "Cora's Room." Sweet Angel Band and Other Stories. Kansas City: Helicon Nine Editions, 1991. 69 – 76.

An adult daughter tries to regain her former love for her aging mother when she returns home in this story but instead drifts farther away. Her mother has become so self-centered with her preoccupation with illness and so hungry for socialization that she talks incessantly during her daughter's visit, yet the two of them cannot hold a meaningful conversation. " 'You make me sick,' " Cora finally erupts in frustrated anger. " 'I've got to get the hell out of here before you drive me as crazy as you' " (72 – 73). Unable to bear her mother's company any more than a week, she cuts short her visit and retreats to her lover waiting in Washington, D. C., torn between the urge to stay and the desire to leave her mother but unable to will herself to stop driving.

34. Koger, Lisa. "Structural Changes." Farlanburg Stories. New York: W. W. Norton, 1990. 205 – 234.

The aging mother in this story tries to direct the life of her 38-year-old daughter, but becomes dismayed when she learns that she has no more control over her daughter's life choices than she does over the signs of her own approaching senility. Although her daughter's "largeness of person" ("Margaret looked like the type of woman who would be good at building fence"), and immaturity disappoint her mother, Eva finds "hope and possibility" in the fact that her daughter is at last doing something positive with her life by attending college part-time. Eva views her daughter's decision to attend college as at least a step toward the fulfillment of her own goals:

> Even if Margaret never learned enough to paint a picture good enough to give to relatives or to hang in the living room, Eva hoped college would result in remarriage for her daughter and grandbabies galore for herself. She craved the chatter of children on her place. She could die a happy woman, she often thought, if only she could hold the sixth generation in her arms. (214)

But Margaret refuses to fit neatly into her mother's prescribed mold, choosing instead to define her own life's choices. Losing control over the direction of her daughter's life, even as she senses her mental acuity slipping away, Eva retreats into her own world of dreams where she is at last safely in complete command. "Here was a world she recognized, and she was impressed by the orderliness of it" (234).

35. Konecky, Edith. "Turn Your Back and Walk Away." The Best College Writing 1961. Ed. Story Magazine. New York: Random House, 1961. 97 – 108.

A daughter's private anguish and guilty feelings for placing her aging mother in a nursing home are examined in this award-winning story, written by a Columbia University student. Jane knows her mother's words are true—"I'll never get better here," she expresses her fears to her daughter—but Jane cannot bring her mother home without angering her husband, who insists that her condition would be the same regardless of where she lives. Yet with each visit, Jane sees undeniable signs of her mother's deterioration:

> Each day, because there was nothing to see, there was a little less vision; because there was nothing to hear, her hearing dulled; because there was no power left to her, her strength diminished. The losses were gradual, the retreat was inevitable. (102)

As Jane tries to straighten her mother's gnarled fingers "in a wistful denial of time," she thinks of how powerful yet gentle those hands once were and all the things her mother once represented as "the source of so much, reward and punishment, nourishment and succor, yes and no, denial, and love, fear and calm, thunder and peace and comfort" (103).

When Jane departs and her mother once more retreats into her own private place of loneliness, she silently begs her mother for forgiveness, for deserting her with so little in life to look forward to, for not being able to reverse time and change the circumstances of their lives.

36. Kornblatt, Joyce Reiser. "Ordinary Mysteries." Nothing to Do With Love. New York: Viking Press, 1981. 189 – 197.

The aging mother slowly recovering from a seizure in this first-person narrative struggles to regain her health and independence, shocking her adult daughter at her adamant refusal to be placed in a nursing home or in the care of a companion, even though her condition has left her physically helpless. When her own mother was close to death, the narrator remembers praying for her death, rationalizing her hopes as an act of mercy. "But I knew," she writes, "it was my own deliverance as much as hers that I sought, and when she slipped away, I was as dizzied by release as by grief" (195). Now her own daughter is caught in a similar situation. "As if she has been kidnapped, this illness of mine has ripped her out of her world and tied her to my sudden helplessness," the mother realizes (195). But as soon as her condition improves slightly, the mother begins to envision herself tending to her own garden and fruit trees once again as a "deep restlessness, a growing sense of imprisonment" propels her forward, even before her body cooperates and allows her to move. "Reason tells me I ought to agree," with her daughter's suggestion, the mother admits, "but reason, after all is just a shadow of life's form: I've always been after the *substance* of things" (196 – 197). The tenacious individuality and independent nature of this aging mother leave her daughter with difficult options for her mother's care and a discomforting uncertainty about how her decisions will affect their relationship.

37. Krasno, Francine. "Celia." Lesbian Fiction: An Anthology. Ed. Elly Bulkin. Watertown, MA: Persephone Press, 1981. 245 – 254.

The Jewish daughter who narrates this story attempts to extract family history from her aging mother before she dies. Considering her own mother a failure, she longs to hear the stories of her grandmother and greatgrandmother. "I want to know what they have done so I will know what is possible for myself," she writes (245). "My greatest fear," she confides, "has been that I would grow to be like my mother: passive, discontented, confined. I want to know if there has been a time in her life when she was not all of these things. I want to find something to like in her. Which will be something to like in myself. Perhaps in my maternal history there is one story that is my own" (246). The stories the mother tells are full of "long journeys and suffering, qualities of endurance and determination. An unbroken thread. Then there are the snags, the life stopped behind a sewing machine, smothered ambitions, hopeless complaints in a sterile ghost room. A mixed birthright" (254). Among the stories there is not a single one of promise "that I can carry away with me like a favorite stone," the daughter laments. What the daughter does take with her is an understanding of her mother that has replaced contempt and the realization that in establishing her own identify separate from her mother and in learning to love herself, "I could let myself love her. A little" (253).

38. Kumin, Maxine. "West." The Ploughshares Reader: New Fiction for the Eighties. Ed. DeWitt Henry. Wainscott, NY: Pushcart Press, 1985. 314 – 322.

"West" is a sensitive character sketch of a woman learning to accept her aging body and adjust to the role of widow, even as she loses two daughters to adulthood at the same time. Choosing to spend the remainder of her life on a rural Maine farm, Lena carves an identity for herself while she relishes memories of those times when her daughters were closer and more dependent upon their mother. Although Lena has hired a young woman to help with the chores of the farm, Evvie fails to fill the void Lena's own daughters have left in her life with their pursuit of separate lives. While Lena allows herself to indulge in memories of her past family, memories that are admittedly modified and sometimes even invented to glorify her mother-daughter relationships, Lena also strives to develop a sense of self apart from her maternal role, changing and inevitably waning as she ages.

39. Moffat, Mary Jane. "Giving My Mother a Bath." My Mother's Daughter: Stories by Women. Ed. Irene Zahava. Freedom, CA: The Crossing Press, 1991. 92 – 103.

An adult daughter and her 78-year-old mother recall events of their past in this story as the daughter lovingly and very carefully bathes her mother's fragile, wrinkled body following a hip replacement operation. The narrator remembers how she squirmed as a child when her mother used the "rough kiss of her spit on a hankie when she rubbed soot from my cheeks" (93). Now it is the daughter who has assumed the role of bather. Without resistance her mother "submits to my soaping;" the daughter-narrator writes, "her very pores seem open to whatever may come" (93). The bathing ritual reminds the narrator of the time when her mother was younger and she sat on the toilet lid to be near her mother as she bathed before going to work. "She was thin then," her daughter remembers. "Her full breasts rode high above the water line. Her lovely lopsided grin revealed her own teeth. When she kissed me goodbye, she smelled of Blue Grass, not the faint, dank vapors of age. She was never sick. And she was never, ever going to die" (101). Now the daughter cannot escape the truth that her aging mother will eventually die, and their bathing routine becomes a bonding ceremony for both mother and daughter.

40. Morris, Mary. "Death Apples." The Bus of Dreams. Boston: Houghton Mifflin, 1985. 193 – 208.

An aging mother experiences a rejuvenation for life and renewed bonding with her daughter when they spend their vacation together on a Caribbean island in this story. Recovering from the trauma of several family deaths and a divorce, Mrs. Hoffman accepts her daughter's invitation to travel together as an opportunity for healing her psychological wounds. But the renewed sexuality and sense of adventure Mrs. Hoffman experiences during their vacation are not only therapeutic but revitalizing as well, if not surprising to her daughter. As the two drive their mopeds to a nearby island to try snorkeling ("Mrs. Hoffman had been a housewife all her life and had never seen the bottom of the sea"), the women seem more like sisters than mothers and daughters in their quest for new experiences (208).

41. Nunes, Susan. "A Moving Day." Stories From the American Mosaic: The Graywolf Annual Seven. Ed. Scott Walker. St. Paul: Graywolf Press, 1990. 130 – 137.

The Japanese-American daughter who narrates this story records her observations and reactions as she witnesses her aging mother shed her past as well as many possessions symbolic of her culture. As the "tiny and fragile" 70-year-old woman sorts through her lifelong possessions as a "last accounting" of her life before she moves into a home for the aged, she is comforted with the thought that "at the very least, she'll not be a burden" to her two grown daughters (130). "We know," the narrator describes the reactions of her sister and herself, "there is a message in all this activity, but we don't know what it is.

Still, we search for it in the odd carton, between layers of tissue paper and silk. We open drawers, peer into the recesses of cupboards, rummage through the depths of closets. What a lot of stuff! We lift, untuck, unwrap, and set aside. The message is there, we know. But what is it? Perhaps if we knew, then we wouldn't have to puzzle out our mother's righteous determination to shed the past" (131). A rich history stands behind each object the mother has piled high for the taking, the selected inheritance for the daughters much larger than the few possessions the mother has chosen to keep. Although the stories behind these objects form a rich mosaic of a woman and her cultural heritage, the daughter realizes that the meanings contained within these treasures "have somehow escaped us in the growing up and growing old" (137). As the mother leaves behind her past to prepare for her eventual death, her daughters inherit an uncertain wealth of memory and culture to attempt to understand and appreciate.

42. Perkins, Fionna. "The Changes." When I Am An Old Woman I Shall Wear Purple. Ed. Sandra Martz. Manhattan Beach, CA: Papier-Mache Press, 1987. 38 – 53.

This story details the recollections of the 15-year-old narrator who witnesses her mother committed to an asylum by her family because of her strange behavior during menopause. When the mother collapses from exhaustion after she stops eating and drinking in response to a vision she says was sent from God, her family agrees to place her in a mental institution. " 'We don't have money for her anywhere else,' " the narrator's older sister explains the rationale of their decision. " 'She's in the change. It's what happens to women then; they go insane. We just did what's best' " (51). But only the daughter-narrator knows her mother's vision was merely a fantasy, similar to many of her own, instead of a sign of insanity. "Didn't they understand that Mother's vision wasn't real, that it was just something she'd imagined like my trips around the world being rich and famous?" she wonders (52).

43. Phillips, Jayne Anne. "Home." Black Tickets. New York: Delacorte Press, 1979. 7 – 25.

The sexual attitudes of an aging mother and her adult daughter are sharply contrasted in this short story. While the daughter openly admits her sexual needs, despite her mother's disapproval of her liberal attitude, her divorced mother represses and denies her sexuality because it would complicate the simplicity of her chosen lifestyle (a life based upon watching television, knitting, and skimming Readers Digest after work each night) to admit those needs. Besides, she asks her daughter, " 'Who would have me?' " sagging and wrinkled. Their conflicting views draw to a climatic head when the daughter makes love to a male friend in a bedroom of her mother's house. " 'I heard you, I heard it,' " her mother accuses. " 'Here, in my own house. Please, how much can you expect me to take?' " (25). This confrontation solidifies the antagonism that has grown between a mother and daughter who are generations apart in sexual attitudes and openness.

44. Sanford, Annette. "Standing By." Lasting Attachments. Dallas: Southern Methodist University Press, 1989. 141 – 151.

A daughter offers physical and emotional support to her 80-year-old mother in this story as the mother undergoes a common ritual of aging—the extraction of her four remaining natural teeth and replacement with dentures. "The problem has been that my mother is still beautiful," writes the daughter-narrator. "Her skin and white hair complement each other superbly. Humor brightens her eyes. Her chin is amazingly firm, her expression joyous. Only these last four teeth, disloyal at a time when loyalty means everything, threaten to deny her cherished hope that her looks will last as long as her life" (142). Dreading the pain of this operation and uncertain how it will affect her appearance, the mother has tried to prepare herself and her daughter for any eventuality. "We all have our roles in this drama of extraction," writes her daughter. "I am the Sustainer. Dr. Fitzpatrick is the Executor. Mother is the Courageous Victim. For weeks we have been readying ourselves" (143). The daughter maintains her supportive role through the successful operation and on into the recovery period. As she watches her mother resting peacefully at home, however, she realizes that eventually she must prepare for a more difficult role to come when she will become the bereaved daughter at the time of her mother's death. She writes:

> I stand over her for a minute, considering how fragile the illusion of her beauty is. In repose, her eyes sink back into the hollow of their sockets, flesh sags away from her jaws. In the shaded light her skin appears sallow; her lips form a thin line that barely emits a flutter of breath.
>
> While I wait for her to wake up, I walk through the rooms of the house, inspecting their quiet, testing myself against the silence, practicing. (151)

45. Spaulding, Carol Vivian. "Not if, when." <u>The Luxury of Tears: Winning Stories from the National Society of Arts and Letters Competition</u>. Ed. Susan Marie Greenburg. Little Rock: August House, 1989. 30 – 43.

A daughter's allegiance to her aging mother as the mother's health begins to deteriorate is contrasted to her sister's indifference toward her mother in this story. The one-legged mother who faces the inevitability of the loss of her remaining leg "any day now" becomes a child herself who is almost totally dependent upon others. But only one of her daughters is willing to assume the maternal role necessary to provide for her mother's care, sacrificing her personal life, while her sister continues her own active social life, disregarding the continuing needs of her mother and the burden borne by her sister.

46. Thomas, Annabel. "Loaves and Fishes." <u>The Phototropic Woman</u>. Iowa City: University of Iowa Press, 1981. 32 – 41.

This story examines the relationship of a daughter caring for her aged mother, who takes for granted the affections of her daughter while she refuses to acknowledge that her favorite child has been dead for 20 years. Aileen cares dutifully and selflessly for her mother, even though she realizes she will never hold the special place in her mother's life that her deceased brother did—her mother's first born and only son, her "manchild." While Aileen patiently but persistently attempts to keep her mother interested in living in the present, her mother's mind vacillates between the reality of now and the recurring fantasy that "Kenny would swing around the bend in the road any time now" (33).

47. Thomas, Audrey. "Sunday Morning, June 4, 1989." The Wild Blue Yonder. Toronto: Penguin Books, 1990. 189 – 200.

While historical events such as the killings in Tiananmen Square in China, the death of Ayatollah, Khomeini in Iran, and the spread of the AIDS virus are occurring in the outside world, the adult daughter in this story listens to the fears expressed during a long distance telephone conversation with her 92-year-old mother that her own, personal world may collapse as she faces possible eviction from her apartment. It is with mixed feelings that Pauline responds to the predicament of her mother. A part of her wants to react patiently and sympathetically to her mother's needs as "she tries to think what she can do to help her mother, who is old, who is lonely, who has never ever been able to make friends, who has a genius in the other direction. For making enemies" (198). The other part of Pauline, however, resents her mother's self-centeredness and lack of awareness of global events occurring around her that are threatening world peace. "She wanted to shout at her mother to get off the phone and turn on the television for Christ's sake, have a look at the larger pain and misery in the world. She wanted to ask, mother, have you ever risked your life? But her mother's personal misery was what was real to her" (199) Although Pauline realizes her mother has never known happiness during her lifetime and "would no doubt go to her grave, or her furnace, if she didn't change her mind again, thinking life had somehow given her the short end of the stick," she knows her mother doesn't deserve to be forced into a "Home (what a misnomer!)" either. Pauline promises to aid her mother's plight, even as her mother abruptly hangs up the telephone receiver while Pauline is offering her help, and Pauline realizes with revealing insight that in twenty years she has never memorized her mother's telephone number.

48. Thompson, Sandra. "Ashes." Close-Ups. Athens: University of Georgia Press, 1984. 49 – 56.

The narrator of this story uses flashbacks of childhood memories intermingled with present images of her relationship with her mother to examine the frustrations of an adult daughter attempting to revive her middle-aged mother's interest in living while her mother gradually wills herself to die. The tall and beautiful woman she remembers who consoled but did not scold her five-year-old daughter when urine unexpectedly ran down her leg in the middle of the night has been replaced by a dark and thin woman with brittle bones and half-closed eyes who chain smokes and whose coffee mug is constantly filled with red wine in the morning and bourbon during the afternoons. The daughter attempts to break the self-defeating monotony of her mother's day with a trip to the beauty parlor, in hopes that if her mother "can do this one thing, perhaps she can do another harder thing, and another" and eventually come out of her self-imposed hibernation from the world (52). But at the last minute, huddled in the corner of the room, silent and unmoving, her mother refuses to leave the house, her eyes saying the thoughts she cannot being herself to verbalize to her daughter: "*Please leave me alone to die. Please, I don't ask you for much*" (54). At the same time the daughter's thoughts, too, are unspoken but painfully weighed: "*You are my mother and you must not die like this. You owe me that much*" (55). By cancelling her mother's hair appointment, the daughter reluctantly concedes to her mother's desire to be left alone to die, realizing that her efforts to revive her mother's interest in living have failed and that she is powerless to change the direction of her mother's life.

3

Alienation

INTRODUCTION

It is not surprising that the theme of mother-daughter alienation has created the longest chapter in this bibliography, for the mother-daughter relationship is often beset by conflicts that cannot be resolved, causing anguish for both mother and daughter. Undoubtedly, many daughters have felt similarly to the adult daughter in Susan Kenney's award-winning "Facing Front" who finds herself lying in bed in the room right next to her mother's, both of them awake, but neither one able to talk to the other because an awkward wall of silence stands between them. "She's inaccessible, out of reach," writes the daughter-narrator in frustration. "I can't talk to her, I've never talked to her about anything that mattered, about her illness, about how I felt; it's always been just like this, the wall between us and the two of us lying here, each in our own separate distress" (28). Other women may identify with Anahid in Margaret Kahn's "Understanding the Enemy" who compares her relationship with her mother to the experience of walking along a river that has "no bridges, no fordable spots, no ferries. Her mother was on one side and she was on the other" (34). In her story "Come Fly With Me," Patricia Volk actually creates a term to describe mother-daughter alienation. She calls it "distancing" and defines it as a frustrated mother who feels abandoned by her daughter might:

> Distancing is what happens when your daughter no longer confides in you. Distancing is what happens when your daughter no longer starts sentences with, Guess what happened to me today? Or, I have a problem. Or, What do you think Ma, huh? Distancing is the erosion of a relationship. It is marked by extreme politeness. It starts with crumbs, like having to get off the phone in a hurry for a flawless reason and ends in hunks like not being able to show up for a birthday or Thanksgiving. (198 – 199)

Once distancing sets in, daughters are no longer able to confide in their mothers. Their lives, once shared so closely with their mothers, become "sealed like cornerstones," Volk writes. They even refuse to argue.

Adolescent daughters vacillating between childhood and adulthood often feel alienated from their mothers. The protagonist of Vera Randal's "Waiting for Jim" who finds herself in an awkward trap between childhood and adulthood experiences the frustration of this kind of alienation. While Nancy experiences an intense yearning for independence and sexual maturity, she feels an equally strong need to remain a child under the protection of her mother. Similarly, mothers can also feel alienated from their adolescent daughters during this difficult period of their lives. The mother in Lucile Vaughn Payne's "The Alien" shocks herself when she first openly admits that her adolescent daughter has turned into "a monster"; only when she confides in another mother and learns that both of them are experiencing similar frustrations raising their adolescent daughters does she find comfort in the knowledge that she is not alone.

The emotional strain of maintaining the mother-daughter bond during adolescence is perhaps best illustrated in Joyce Carol Oates's "Heat." In desperation the mother in this story plans a shopping trip, hoping to reestablish closeness with her daughter. But the effort only proves exhausting for each of them, the daughter hiding away in her own self-absorbed world, a place where mothers of teenaged daughters are not allowed to go. Similarly, the mother in Kate Braverman's "Virgin of Tenderness" attempts to grow closer to her adolescent daughter as they travel to eastern Europe to find their ancestral roots. But Heather remains sullen and indifferent to the personal and historical significance of the journey to her mother, her preoccupation with herself is so all encompassing. The mother in Lucile Vaughn Payne's "The Alien" begins to doubt her own mothering ability when her adolescent daughter turns into a moody, irritable, distant, unpredictable "monster." When she confides her frustrations to another mother of a teenaged daughter, the mother assures her she is not alone. " 'You scratch any modern female with a teen-age daughter and you find a woman on the edge of hysterics,' " she consoles (75).

The alienation which separates mother and daughter often results from conflicting attitudes and values, the mother feeling betrayed because her daughter has forsaken the lifestyle she envisioned for her daughter and chosen her own independent path instead. This is especially apparent in Paulette Bates Alden's "Ladies' Luncheon." Miriam is a disappointment to her mother because she fails to fit the model of the perfect Southern woman who proudly exemplifies all the prescribed ingredients in her demeanor: "gentility, kindness, sweetness, the sanctity of God and family, bridge and sherry, the beach and maids" (51). By moving away from her South Carolina homeland, Miriam leaves behind the prescribed notions of womanhood which still prevail in the South. When she adopts a nontraditional lifestyle based upon individuality rather than convention, Miriam alienates herself from a disappointed and confused mother. In other stories authored by Merrill Joan Gerber, Vanessa Howard, Ellen Wilbur, and Helen Hull, conflicting mother-daughter attitudes toward wedding ceremonies, civil rights activism, materialism, and lesbianism alienate mothers and daughters.

Efforts of mothers to control their daughters' behavior result in alienation in several of these stories. In an extreme case, the Jewish mother in Sheila Schwartz's "Passover" continues to formulate solutions to her daughter's problems and manufacture possible suitors, even after Shira enters college. Her assault is so relentless that Shira begins to contemplate suicide as the only possible escape. The 35-year-old virgin in Maureen Howard's "Bridgeport Bus" finally breaks the maternal bond she feels is not only controlling her life, but gradually devouring it. She and her mother "eat each other over the years," the narrator explains, "tender morsel by morsel, until there is nothing left but dry bone and wig," just as warriors once ate the hearts of their enemies (240). The nine-year-old daughter in Amy Tan's "Rules of the Game" tolerates three years of pressure from her mother to become a champion chess player before she explodes in defiance, boldly challenging her mother: " 'Why do you have to use me to show off? If you want to show off, then why don't you learn to play chess?' " (166).

Cultural differences can also cause mother-daughter alienation. The Norwegian-American mother in Borghild Dahl's "from Homecoming" and the Chinese-American mother in Gish Jen's "The White Umbrella" both resent their daughters inevitable drifting away from their native cultures as they become Americanized. The Japanese-American daughter in R. A. Sasaki's "Seattle" rejects her mother's traditional idea of a mother-daughter relationship based upon a "bond of obligation, of suffering, of love" where there must be suffering and sacrifice (112). The daughter in Vickie L. Sears's "Keeping Sacred Secrets" clings to her dead father's Native American heritage despite her mother's attempts to force her to conform to an Anglo world. A black daughter in Alice Walker's "Everyday Use" alienates herself from her sister as well as her mother when she dismisses the traditional lifestyle and values of her family, changes her name, and becomes an activist for the future of her race. The American daughter in Maria Thomas's "The Visit" becomes alienated from her mother when she moves to Africa and chooses to assimilate into the Nigerian culture which her mother finds too exotic and primitive for her taste. The Native American mother and daughter in Anna Lee Walters's "Apparitions" experience a collective alienation from the Anglo world when they encounter hostility and racial prejudice during a shopping trip in a predominantly white town.

Marriage alienates mother and daughter in Tess Slesinger's "Mother to Dinner." Torn between the love she feels for her husband and her equally intense feelings of abandonment of her mother, the daughter in this story feels like a "human shuttle" who vacillates between the two people who mean the most in her life but who unfortunately feel antagonistic toward one another. Katherine feels free to be neither totally wife nor daughter since her decision to marry.

Motherhood itself alienates a mother and daughter in Merrill Joan Gerber's "A Daughter of My Own." When a mother comes to help her daughter care for her new granddaughter, her desire to control the household and her intrusion upon her daughter's privacy spoils the daughter's vision of an idyllic homecoming. "If I never have another baby," the narrator confesses, "it won't be because I didn't like being pregnant or being in labor or losing six-month's worth of sleep—it will be because I won't know what to do about my mother" (220).

Mental instability of mothers is the cause of alienation separating mothers and daughters in stories written by Joyce Carol Oates, Christine Schutt, and Susan Kenney. Daughters in these stories grow up deprived of a loving and supportive relationship with their mothers. The daughter in Oates's "Matter and Energy" suffers from longtime trauma as well after she witnesses her deranged mother trying to commit suicide.

While some of these writers foresee hope for mother-daughter reconciliation in their stories, still others predict no chance to heal this broken bond. Fictions written by Mary Caponegro, Anais Nin, Karen Brennan, and Susan Kenney remind us that if the mother-daughter bond is fractured during childhood, it may not be restored later. For the daughter in Nin's "A Slippery Floor" the desire to be as unlike her estranged mother as possible becomes a guiding force her in development as a woman and her choice of a dancing career. While the adult daughter in Roxanna Robinson's "The Time for Kissing" regrets all the intimate conversations that she and her mother will never have after her emotionally distant mother announces, at the age of 71, that she is no longer kissing people, the adult daughter in Kenney's "Facing Front" experiences a sense of relief when her relationship with her equally distant mother comes to an impasse. She accepts the fact with a certain peace that it is fruitless to attempt to fabricate a relationship where one has never existed. Exasperated in her attempts to reestablish a bond with her mother for the first time, the adult daughter in Suzanne Zuhasz's "Make Believe I Love You" imagines a conversation with her mother in which she criticizes her for the self-centeredness that has prevented their closeness for so many years. In her mind she tells her mother:

> "I turn myself to stone. I show nothing on my face. You throw your words against me and they bounce right back at you. I won't let you near. I won't let you in. I refuse to give you anything that is me. I have to protect myself. You take everything and turn it back into you ." (41–42)

Marsha Portnoy, Arny Christine Straayer, Andrea Barrett, Barbara Kingsolver, and Kathleen Spivack are among a minority of women writers who envision hope for alienated mothers and daughters in their stories. Unlike the mother and daughter in Gerber's story who drift apart when the daughter also becomes a mother herself, the mothers and daughters in Portnoy's "Loving Strangers" and Kathleen Spivack's "Generations" grow closer together through this mutual experience. For the first time the daughter-narrator of "Loving Strangers" can remember, her outwardly perfect mother reveals herself as an individual capable of failure and imperfection. At the same time that this admission of truth humanizes her mother, it gives the daughter hope that the two of them can become more than "distant strangers." Mother and daughter take awkward but initial steps to heal their wounded relationship in Straayer's "High Heels" after the adolescent daughter is released from a psychiatric hospital where she was committed by her mother for being unmanageable. An estranged mother and daughter in Barbara Kingsolver's "Islands on the Moon" gradually begin to mend their relationship when they both simultaneously approach motherhood for the second time. " 'We're like islands on the moon,' " the mother tells her daughter. " 'A person could walk from one to the other if they just decided to do it' " (146).

SHORT FICTION

49. Alden, Paulette Bates. "Ladies' Luncheon." Feeding the Eagles. St. Paul: Graywolf Press, 1988. 45 – 61.

    The invisible power mothers continue to wield over their adult daughters, even those who have distanced themselves and carved their own identities, is illustrated in this story. The daughter-protagonist of this story who returns to her childhood South Carolina home feels smothered by her mother's persistent questioning of her lifestyle and her inability to accept her daughter's individuality. Unlike several of her high school friends, whom her mother continues to hold before her daughter as exemplars of social acceptability, Miriam does not fit the model of the perfect Southern woman who has all the proper ingredients: "gentility, kindness, sweetness, the sanctity of God and family, bridge and sherry, the beach and maids" (51). Following a "ladies' luncheon" where Miriam is the obvious social misfit among her former classmates who are perfect examples of Southern ladies, she escapes from her mother's scrutiny to the basement of her former home where she can finally let her strained face relax "and assume its human shape" once more, where she can enjoy being herself in private. Should she fly back to Minnesota early or somehow endure the last three days of her scheduled visit, she wonders. To stay is to risk further alienation from her mother, but to depart now would leave the inevitable reconciliation to dread later— the apologies and hurt feelings. "How much power her mother has! Still! Miriam would have thought she was beyond it" (61). Not even adamantly independent daughters who have moved north, forsaken Southern tradition, postponed motherhood, read Plato, and smoked marijuana can escape the power of their own mothers, Alden's narrative reminds readers.

50. Barrett, Andrea. "The Church of No Reason." American Voices: Best Short Fiction by Contemporary Authors. Ed. Sally Arteseros. New York: Hyperion, 1992. 277 – 292.

This story examines the causes of conflict which alienate a mother from her daughters before they are reunited and the mother-daughter bond is restored. When the mother of the story loses her second husband to his bookkeeper, she begins to practice a mystical religion that allows her mind to transcend reality. So distracted by her loss is she that she provides her children with minimal structure and no disciplinary boundaries, although their behavior clearly begs for control. By the time their mother is hospitalized as a result of a mental breakdown, her daughters have become juvenile delinquents. When she does return, changed if not healed, the mother and her daughters begin the process of reestablishing a bond of trust and care once again while the mother gradually recuperates

51. Bingham, Sallie. "Please No Eating No Drinking." The Way It Is Now. New York: Viking Press, 1972. 109 – 117.

The distance between a mother and her daughter in this story is particularly alarming because the mother is unaware of its presence until her daughter's life becomes endangered. Relieved to be divorced from her husband after 20 years of what she terms "hard labor," Louise relishes the freedom of living alone with her only daughter, a high school senior. Although Louise acknowledges that Katy has a weight problem, she takes pleasure in her daughter's "quiet and purposeful" ways and her undemanding nature. Only when Louise accidentally discovers that her daughter is a drug abuser does she begin to realize how little she really knows her daughter and how unaware she has been of her daughter's apparent unhappiness while she has been engrossed in her own social life and career.

52. Brady, Maureen. "Corsage." My Mother's Daughter: Stories by Women. Ed. Irene Zahava. Freedom, CA: The Crossing Press, 1991. 161 – 171.

A daughter rejects a gift symbolic of her mother's love and pride in this story because to accept it would undoubtedly mean social rejection by her peers. When Leslie's mother learns that her daughter is to receive an academic award, she brings a corsage to school for her daughter to wear during the presentation. Even though she knows that not accepting the corsage will hurt her mother's feelings, Leslie refuses to wear it because "nobody wears a corsage around here, except for prom and we already had that last week" (166). By rejecting the corsage Leslie puts her own social status among her classmates ahead of her relationship with her mother.

53. Braverman, Kate. "Virgin of Tenderness." Squandering the Blue. New York: Fawcett Columbine, 1990. 207 – 221.

When a recurrence of cancer threatens the life of a mother in this story, she visits her eastern European roots with her adolescent daughter as a pilgrimage into time and identity. While the trip expands Maggie's consciousness of time and her cultural heritage, it alienates her further from her daughter, whose concept of what is important in life has been narrowed by the self-interest that often dominates adolescence. Sullen and indifferent to the personal and historical significance of the journey to her mother, Heather views this trip as yet another of her mother's self-centered attempts to "stand center stage and suck up all the air" (215). Maggie's discoveries about herself and the larger scope of mankind found in the ancient ruins of eastern Europe are savored alone, for she recognizes and accepts the realization that to attempt to share these revelations with her daughter at this phase in her youthful life would be futile.

54. Brennan, Karen. "Cooking the Geography of Distance." Wild Desire. Amherst: University of Massachusetts Press, 1991. 82 – 86.

The entire plot of this story takes place during a mother-daughter telephone conversation. Seeking advice and consolation as she contemplates divorce, the daughter calls her mother, but the maternal advice she receives only widens the distance that already exists between them. The daughter writes in despair: "Oh you want to do whatever's noble & she says you're an idealist, a kind of female spoiler, a variety of sea-bug, get with it, buy more high heels, get an organ or two carved out before life passes you by the way a bus passes a condemned municipal building or a gum wrapper—" (86).

55. Brennan, Karen. "Daughter." Wild Desire. Amherst: University of Massachusetts Press, 1991. 47 – 49.

A mother's worst nightmare is reenacted in this fantasy. Brennan places each reader in the role of the mother-protagonist, eating chocolates while watching soap operas in bed, who bemoans the quick passage of time that has robbed her of a toddler and left her with an unwed, pregnant daughter who is also a drug addict and prostitute as well. As the daughter rummages in her mother's closet and emerges wearing her Chinese robe and brandishing a sharp, bread knife, she lunges at the reader as well, ready to fulfill the role of every mother's worst nightmare of a daughter. "In the robe," Brennan sets the tragic scene for her readers, "your daughter resembles a giant embroidered bat, flapping and flapping. She moves toward you with the knife. You close your eyes. You always knew this would happen" (49).

56. Brennan, Karen. "Polio." Wild Desire. Amherst: University of Massachusetts Press, 1991. 35 – 40.

Narrated alternately from the viewpoint of the daughter narrator and an omniscient narrator, this innovative story explores the special bond that exists between a mother and her terminally ill son and the effect their close relationship has upon the seven-year-old daughter of the family. Feeling neglected by her mother, whose attention was absorbed by her brother during their childhood, the daughter writes that as a child she felt as if "she was a huge wooden object that had intruded into a tiny exquisite world" (40).

57. Brown, Mary Ward. "It Wasn't All Dancing." New Stories from the South: The Year's Best, 1989. Ed. Shannon Ravenel. Chapel Hill: Algonquin Books, 1989. 202 – 214.

Although the daughter in this story never makes an appearance, her presence is felt strongly, for she now controls the care of her aging mother and determines whether or not she will be placed in a nursing home. While her daughter was growing up, the mother confesses to her favorite among a series of nurses hired and fired by her daughter, " 'I was no mother, to anybody. I was out being the belle of the ball myself. I went off and left her with any black woman who'd sleep on a cot in her room. She has every reason to feel the way she does toward me' " (209). What her daughter remembers most about her, the mother imagines, was the scent of "Chanel Number Five as I went out the door, then alcohol and cigarettes when I came in her room late at night . . . " (209). Now her daughter avoids contact with her, carefully visiting at times when her mother is asleep, and makes decisions about her care from afar. Because she cannot reverse her past mistakes, the mother in this story can only hope for forgiveness from her estranged daughter, in whose control her life has now been unavoidably placed.

58. Caponegro, Mary. "Materia Prima." The Star Cafe and Other Stories. New York: Charles Scribner's Sons, 1990. 47 – 87.

A mother who never learned how to develop a close relationship with her daughter during her childhood tries too late to rebuild an intimate bond in this innovative story that is written as part-narrative, part-stream-of consciousness-prose, and part-drama. By the time her mother tries to reach her daughter, Clara has withdrawn into her own world of profound separateness and has become a "veiled child, distant child, never content to be just a child, insisting on adult traits, and demanding to know what children cannot know," an anorexic child who stops eating out of loneliness and isolation (82). Only in her solitary dreams and reading does Clara discover "solace" and a "glimpse of liberation" from the "irreconcilable alienation" that now governs her life (73).

59. Crane, Moira. "Cleanliness." The Winnebago Mysteries and Other Stories. New York: Fiction Collective, 1982. 47 – 53.

The youngest of three adult daughters in this story, who claims to be her mother's "worst and last daughter" and certainly the most disappointing of the three, fantasizes a visit from her mother that transforms itself into a surrealistic nightmare. A woman who "was as distant as a photographed angel" from her daughters as they were growing up and she was devoting her energies to becoming rich instead of concentrating on motherhood, the mother of three remains emotionally distant and judgmental. "Whenever she visits her daughters," the narrator writes, "heaven is in the room disapproving" (49). During this imaginary visit fantasized by the youngest daughter, the mother is portrayed as clearly uncomfortable in her daughter's modest and less-than-meticulous surroundings. She grows hysterical when she slips on furnace grease in the basement of the house and sustains a hideous brown stain on the thigh of her white pants. While the narrator rushes to the nearest store, purchasing every brand of cleaning agent in sight, her mother cleans the entire basement to perfection, even as she grows larger and larger, gradually becoming a part of the house itself. The daughter feels an elated sense of cleansing and freedom when she returns to witness this bizarre happening as she observes her mother and her house gradually becoming one entity.

60. Dahl, Borghild. "from Homecoming." The Minnesota Experience: An Anthology. Ed. Jean Ervin. Minneapolis: Adams Press, 1979. 255 – 269.

    In this novel excerpt, a Norwegian-American daughter defies her mother by sneaking away from home to attend a Christmas church service with an American friend, even though her mother has forbidden the visit, terrified that her daughter will become "Yankeefied" and reject her Norwegian heritage for less desirable American ways. It is Lyng's grandmother who intercedes and prevents her mother from severely punishing her disobedient daughter, reminding her of Lyng's need for independence and assimilation into American culture.

61. Erhart, Margaret. "Mothers, Daughters." My Mother's Daughter: Stories by Women. Ed. Irene Zahava. Freedom, CA: The Crossing Press, 1991. 216 – 224.

    This story explores the motivations that underlie a daughter's eating disorder and her mother's regret at not detecting the problem sooner, as narrated by a second daughter. As Toria refuses all food and will not look directly at her reflection in the mirror, she confides to her sister that she would like to be "flat and light as air" so that she could fly away. Toria's mother berates herself for demonstrating the greatest of all human faults— "the failure to pay attention"—which could have prevented her daughter's unhappiness.

62. Gerber, Merrill Joan. "A Daughter of My Own." Stop Here, My Friend. Boston: Houghton Mifflin, 1965. 220 – 234.

    A mother and daughter become alienated from one another in this story, even as the daughter becomes a mother herself for the first time. Although the narrator insists that she loves her mother, when she comes to help care for her new granddaughter her controlling presence and invasion of her daughter's limited privacy become a source of conflict that spoils the daughter's vision of an idyllic introduction to motherhood. The narrator's mother departs earlier than planned, feeling rejected and unneeded, leaving her daughter with conflicting feelings of grief and remorse. "If I never have another baby," the narrator writes, "it won't be because I didn't like being pregnant or being in labor or losing six-month's worth of sleep—it will be because I won't know what to do about my mother" (220).

63. Gerber, Merrill Joan. "Forty Watts." Stop Here, My Friend. Boston: Houghton Mifflin, 1965. 143 – 159.

A mother experiences confusion and feelings of rejection in this story when her daughter favors a nontraditional wedding and rejects the values she has been taught. The concerns of young people of her daughter's generation, who talk of "bombs and godlessness and free love," are disconcerting to Ruthie's mother, who values tradition and stability. No one has a "firm direction" anymore, she laments, "there was no tradition left, no rules so mighty children couldn't give you big arguments about them" (145). That there is confusion in the world Mrs. Stein can tolerate, but she cannot abide conflict in her relationship with her nonconforming daughter. Although their differing values are a continual source of conflict through the planning and execution of Ruthie's wedding, Ruthie's assurance of love for her mother after the event relieves the fears Mrs. Stein harbors that she has been rejected by her only daughter.

64. Gerber, Merrill Joan. "Stop Here, My Friend." Stop Here, My Friend. Boston: Houghton Mifflin, 1965. 45 – 53.

A 31-year-old daughter takes positive steps toward independence from her protective but dependent mother in this story. Kate has never felt a closeness to her mother, who still treats her as if she were a child, yet insists she is dependent upon her care. When Kate witnesses a mother and daughter obviously enjoying each other's company in a restaurant, the mother occasionally touching her daughter's arm "in a gesture of approval and pride and delight," she realizes that in all of their years together, she and her mother have never laughed together that way. This disturbing scene becomes the stimulus that motivates Kate to hunt for an apartment of her own, acknowledging that she is ready to live independently and that her mother can manage her own life without her constant care.

65. Goldstein, Rebecca. "The Legacy of Raizel Kaidish: A Story." America and I: Short Stories by American Jewish Women Writers. Ed. Joyce Antler. Boston: Beacon Press, 1990. 281 – 289.

A Holocaust survivor's obsession with the moral education of her daughter, born of guilt for her own crime against another woman, gradually alienates her daughter in this story. The narrator explains how she was named after Raizel Kaidish, the "heroine of block eight," who died in the gas chamber at Buchenwald after an informer reported that Raizel planned to trade places with a sick friend whose name had been placed on the death list in hopes that both of them might survive. It is only at the end of the story, when Raizel's mother is on her deathbed, that Raizel learns the dark truth that her own mother was the informer who was rewarded with the prisoner's coveted kitchen position. When Raizel gives birth to her own child, her resentment toward her mother's stringent moral philosophy gradually solidifies into hate. She realizes she "knew what no child should ever know: that my mother had had me for some definite reason and that she would always see me in terms of this reason. I sensed this in my mother, and I hated her for it" (296). Only when Raizel's mother confesses her Holocaust secret does her daughter begin to understand the underlying guilt that is the source of her mother's rigid, moralistic view of life. But by then it is too late, for she has severed whatever emotional ties may have once existed between mother and daughter.

66. Howard, Maureen. "Bridgeport Bus." Prize Stories 1962: The O. Henry Awards. Ed. Richard Poirier. Garden City: Doubleday 1962. 239 – 250.

The 35-year-old virgin who narrates this story finally breaks the maternal bond she feels is devouring her and takes flight from home on her own for the first time. The daughter has lived with her mother for so long that they have become experts at the "cannibal game" they play. "We eat each other over the years," the narrator explains, "tender morsel by morsel, until there is nothing left but dry bone and wig" (240). The mother is winning the game, the daughter concedes, because she has more experience. The daughter knows that if she showed any sympathy toward her mother, it would be an act of self-sacrifice: "I would offer myself to her, the last sweet bite, a soupcon airy and delicious to restore her, humanity fudge. Warriors did that," the narrator explains, "not as long ago as we would like to think—ate the heart of the enemy" (247 – 248). As the narrator departs from home, no clear destination in mind, a myriad of exotic possibilities present themselves as future options now that she has severed the oppressive maternal cord before allowing herself to be completely consumed.

67. Howard, Vanessa. "Let Me Hang Loose." Tales and Stories for Black Folks. Ed. Toni Cade Bambara. Garden City: Doubleday, 1971. 101 – 121.

The 18-year-old black narrator of this story becomes alienated from her mother when she becomes active in the civil rights movement, despite her mother's contention that "it wasn't respectful" to demonstrate. So many times, the narrator remembers in retrospect, "I wanted to scream at her, to shake her until she woke up to the world I was in, " 'Momma, how can I act respectful when I haven't gained respect?' " (101). As the daughter becomes active in the movement—even sustaining a head injury during a race riot—she regrets that she did not defy her mother earlier and becomes more estranged from her, remembering her as "nothing but a wall that stood between me and my Black people, me and life, me and love, and me and happiness" (104). By the time mother and daughter attempt a reconciliation, the narrator lies awaiting her premature death from a drug overdose. The mother's words of support to her daughter, " 'I am with you, not against you' " come too late for a daughter who nevertheless takes comfort that she and her mother stood together at last before she died.

68. Hull, Helen Rose. "The Fire." Women in Literature: Live Stages through Stories, Poems, and Plays. Ed. Sandra Eagleton. Englewood Cliffs: Prentice Hall, 1988. 32 – 40.

A mother's jealousy over her daughter's affections for an older woman alienate mother and daughter in this story. Raised in a home environment of utility and practicality that seems as stifling as a prison at times, Cynthia is attracted to the spontaneity and lack of order she discovers in her art teacher's disheveled life. A visit to Miss Egret's life is an escape from bland predictability into a world of spontaneous art and beauty. But Cynthia's mother forbids her to return to Miss Egret's, feeling obligated to protect her daughter's innocence. Underlying her motives are maternal feelings of rejection and emotional pain that her daughter would prefer the company of a sentimental old maid who sits by the fireside and talks of beauty. " 'You know mother wants just what is best for you, don't you?' " Cynthia's mother assures her. " 'I can't let you drift away from us, your head full of silly notions.' " But the "silly notions" of rebellion and escape have already been planted in Cynthia's mind and because of her mother's intolerance and lack of understanding, their alienation as mother and daughter, too, has been assured.

69. Hull, Helen Rose. "Separation." Last September. Tallahassee: Naiad Press, 1988. 19 – 30.

An adolescent daughter begins to recognize her lesbian identity as she starts to individuate from her mother in this story. Although her mother's attempts to discourage Cynthia's relationship with an older woman in the community succeed, Cynthia's feelings have already been recorded in personal letters for the first time and the ropes binding her, "tying her away from a strange new self which struggled uncouthly within her," have been severed (20). "For the first time she was sharply a person, thrilling with the bitter taste of separation from other people. The frayed ropes which had bound her had broken at last. Something in her no one could touch, could demand—not even her mother" (29). As Cynthia begins to experience the "gleeful, bitter taste of separate identity," knowing for the first time that "she had something which no one could enter, could wrest from her," she moves away from her mother's protection and control to create her own individual identity.

70. Jen, Gish. "The White Umbrella." My Mother's Daughter: Stories by Women. Ed. Irene Zahava. Freedom, CA: The Crossing Press, 1991. 196 – 205.

The Americanization of a Chinese family living in the United States causes conflict between a mother and her two young daughters in this story. While the daughters resent their mother taking a job to help support the family, a practice contrary to Chinese tradition, the mother resents her daughters' desire to more material possessions, which she dismisses as too American. " 'All you want is things,' "she accuses one daughter who longs for an umbrella for Christmas, " 'just like an American' " (199).

71. Juhasz, Suzanne. "Make Believe I Love You." Frontiers 3.2 (1978): 40 – 42.

The adult daughter in this novel excerpt attempts to establish a bond with her mother for the first time but fails because her mother is too preoccupied with self-interest to give the relationship the balance that it needs. Invariably, whenever the two women begin a dialogue, the mother turns the course of the conversation to herself, unleashing a storm of "white cotton padding, unrolling without pause" that keeps her daughter at a distance and protects her against any closeness the two of them might develop. During an imaginary talk with her mother, which eventually and inevitably becomes dominated with the mother's concerns, the daughter finally gives up trying to communicate and announces:

> "I turn myself to stone. I show nothing on my face. You throw your words against me and they bounce right back at you. I won't let you near. I won't let you in. I refuse to give you anything that is me. I have to protect myself. You take everything and turn it back into you." (41 – 42)

The only closeness the daughter remembers experiencing with her mother was when she was a child and secretly listened to her mother's music collection. The romanticized lyrics helped the daughter understand the appeal of the music was her mother's escape from the imprisonment of reality and her own unhappiness into a fantasy world of romantic possibilities. But years later the grown daughter needs more than romantic music lyrics to understand her mother, yet her mother offers no opportunity to create a relationship where one has never existed.

72. Kahn, Margaret. "Understanding the Enemy." Iowa Woman. Spring 1992: 29 – 34.

An American daughter and her Armenian mother remain distant even into the daughter's adulthood in this story because their life experiences have been so drastically different. The mother, who survived massacres and marches and witnessed the death of relatives at the hands of Turks, spends much of her time retelling those nightmares of her past. Her daughter, born safely in the United States, has no recollection of those atrocities except for what she envisions as she listens to her mother's endless stories. Mother and daughter remain distant because the mother cannot forgive her daughter "for having an easier time" in life than she did. "For not having to go on the marches" (34). Had Anahid survived the massacres with her mother, they may have been able to establish a close mother-daughter bond. But building such intimacy seems impossible now. Their relationship "was like walking along the river," it seemed to Anahid. "One that had no bridges, no fordable spots, no ferries. Her mother was on one side and she was on the other" (34).

73. Kenney, Susan. "Facing Front." Prize Stories 1982: The O. Henry Awards. Ed. William Abrahams. Garden City: Doubleday, 1982. 1 – 31.

"Facing Front," which placed first among the O. Henry Award-winning stories for 1982, analyzes a mother-daughter relationship marred by the continued grief and vacillating sanity of a mother widowed early in her marriage and left with three small children. The adult daughter who narrates the story makes repeated attempts to build a closer relationship with a mother who has never been able to vocalize her love for her children. The daughter finally realizes there is a distance separating them that can never be reconciled, no matter how hard she tries. During a visit to her mother's house with her own children, she lies in the room next to her mother's, both of them awake, neither able to bridge the gap separating their lives. "She's inaccessible, out of reach," writes the narrator in frustration. "I can't talk to her, I've never talked to her about anything that mattered, about her illness, about how I felt; it's always been just like this, the wall between us and the two of us lying here, each in our own separate distress" (28). Realizing that the moment of impasse in their relationship has come, the narrator admits to herself: "I've worn out the thin fabric of my unquestioning childhood love, and what is left? There are too many cobwebs here, too many echoes, cries of past and present misery, confusion and despair, and no one sees or hears them but me" (30). There is a certain peace that comes to the daughter with this admission that relieves her from the arduous chore of continuing to attempt to fabricate a relationship with her aging mother where one has never existed.

74. Kingsolver, Barbara. "Islands on the Moon." Homeland and Other Stories. New York: Harper and Row, 1989. 119 – 147.

A 44-year-old mother and her daughter, both unmarried and approaching motherhood for the second time, begin to mend their estranged relationship in this story when a potentially life- threatening automobile accident forces them to confront the fragility of life. Annemarie has always resented her mother's alternative lifestyle and values (During adolescence Magda forced her daughter go to antiwar sit-ins and drink barley fiber while she forbade Annemarie to use hair spray because it depletes the ozone layer) and her overprotective attitude. Although mother and daughter live within walking distance, Annemarie hasn't spoken to her mother for months. Magda says she's willing to wait until Annemarie stops "emitting negative energy toward her" and happily announces her pregnancy to her daughter by mail. " 'We're like islands on the moon,' " Magda tells her daughter. " 'A person could walk from one to the other if they just decided to do it' " (146). The distance between those islands begins to gradually shrink when mother and daughter confess their mutual shortcomings and disappointments as mother and daughter while they are hospitalized together following the accident. They begin to anticipate the future when they will both be new mothers raising their babies together.

75. Kirshenbaum, Bonnie. "Complex." My Mother's Daughter: Stories by Women. Ed. Irena Zahava. Freedom, CA: The Crossing Press, 1991. 50 – 62.

During a shopping trip where the entire plot of this story takes place, a mother seeks to reestablish closeness with her adult daughter, who realizes their differences have become irreconcilable. The mother continues to see her daughter as she would like her to be, not as she is—a manager for a rock band with spiked hair and an aversion to malls ("the postmodern suburban statement"), which her mother finds so wonderfully convenient. The daughter-narrator confides that she won't allow her mother to see her New York City apartment, for its barrenness would surely offend her taste as much as the lover she once brought home named Spark who wore earrings and had his head shaved in spots. Alma expresses concern over the lack of security in her daughter's profession. " 'I worry,' " she confesses to her daughter. " 'I can't help it but I worry. You have no security. What will become of you?' " (59). The story ends with a scene in a restaurant booth where Alma is flipping through her wallet, glancing at pictures of her daughter during earlier, less disconcerting stages of life—"her card catalogue of what was and what could have been"—while the daughter-narrator wonders what her hair would look like dyed aubergine.

76. Kobin, Joann. "The Lost Glove." "Eric Clapton's Lover" and Other Stories from the *Virginia Quarterly Review*. Eds. Sheila McMillen and George Garrett. Charlottesville: University Press of Virginia, 1990. 135 – 146.

This story illustrates how mothers and daughters can feel close to one another but never really know one another. While offering readers their choice of beginnings and endings for this innovative story in the "character" section of her narrative, Kobin portrays the college freshman daughter as intellectually curious and sensitive and her mother as traditional and unfulfilled. Even though Rita accepts Jeanne's invitation to visit Wellesley (as the only parent on campus) and help fill the void of loneliness that has entered her life, she leaves without mother and daughter really communicating. "*Later J. is aware of something unfinished, some omission,*" writes Kobin. "*There was something she didn't say to her mother—or was it a question she forgot to ask?* " (144).

Rita dies in an accident before Jeanne ever sees her mother again. While mourning her mother's death, Jeanne also mourns the fact that she never really knew the mother she has lost. "*The omission: not having asked the right questions, enough questions*" (146).

While both mother and daughter were absorbed in playing their separate roles, these women failed to know one another intimately, their relationship built more upon need and familial ties rather than genuine understanding and caring.

77. Kumin, Maxine. "The Facts of Life." Why Can't We Live Together Like Civilized Human Beings? New York: Viking Press, 1982. 9 – 19.

As the mother who narrates this story awaits the onset of her daughter's menstrual periods, an event both agree should be celebrated, she remembers her own emotionally detached mother and the inadequate preparation for the facts of life and death she was offered as a child. Her mother died a lonely person who was offended by intimacy and spontaneous displays of feeling, who guarded her sense of self-control diligently. It is only after her mother's death that the daughter begins to piece together the events of her mother's life which caused her to remove herself from the affections of other people, including her daughter.

78. Lowe, Bia. "I Always Write About My Mother When I Start to Write." Indivisible: New Short Fiction by West Coast Gay & Lesbian Writers. Eds. Terry Wolverton and Robert Drake. New York: Penguin Books, 1991. 61 – 63.

The lesbian daughter in this story confesses that her first crush on a woman began at the age of four, and the object of her affections was her mother. "She was in every way my female deity," the daughter-narrator writes. "Now every woman in the act of love resembles her. . . " (61). Awed by the sensual allure of her mother, the narrator remembers being "suddenly seized with a desire to court her. To bear gifts as if riding on horseback from some faraway kingdom. I wanted to lay them, breathtaking, at her feet, and by doing so bind her heart to mine, ever after to be buoyed up like a life raft on a calmed ocean" (61). But none of her four-year-old treasures were worthy enough, and her prized offering, a white cup with a rubber band around it, was kindly refused by her mother. This moment of rejection brought the daughter her first taste of "inexpressible loneliness" and remains an influential segment in her life, even though years have past. "Now," the narrator confesses, "every act of writing resembles this, because I must think very hard about what I give people. I want to offer a cup with a rubber band around it and way, this is more than just a cup, take it and we will float up together like that moment in dreams, or that moment I reach for, looking up into the faces of the women I love, from some faraway kingdom, bearing the inexpressible" (63).

79. Newlin, Louisa. "Our Last Day in Venice." Short Stories for Insight. Ed. Teresa Ferster Glazier. New York: Harcourt, Brace and World, 1967. 21 – 28.

A mother and her newly married daughter come to an impasse in this story when the mother refuses to accept her daughter's change in values. Mrs. Bownell has difficulty accepting the fact that her daughter has chosen to marry a painter. Artists, she believes, " 'may be very interesting and creative, but they don't make very good husbands and wives, believe me,' " she tells her daughter (25). She also disapproves of the couple's plans to live in Rome indefinitely. The mother advises her daughter that the best job opportunities for her husband are undoubtedly "back where he has roots" (24). But most unforgivable of all to her mother is Felicity's apparent disinterest with material possessions, which her mother interprets as a sign of personal ingratitude and rejection of her family's values.

80. Nin, Anais. "A Slippery Floor." Waste of Timelessness and Other Early Stories. Weston, CT: Magic Circle Press, 1977. 87 – 105.

A daughter's desire to be as different from her mother as possible prevents them from becoming competitors for the same lover but also severs their newfound relationship in this narrative. Growing up with her father, Anita learns little about her estranged mother other than she "never denied herself any whim, however much it hurt others" (93). Anita vows to "be as unlike my Mother as possible," intentionally choosing a career in dancing, in part, because "from all I heard I gathered it would be the most difficult career in which to practice such a life" (93). When Vivien and her daughter reunite years later and discover they are attracted to the same man, Anita refuses to hurt her mother by accepting his affections, even though Vivien has advised her to let nothing and no one stand in the way of her own search for happiness. But Anita challenges herself to "have the courage to do what her Mother had never done: resist. Resist for the sake of denying herself a happiness which hurt another, resist for the sake of testing herself, of measuring the depths between her character and Vivien's" (104). Although pained by the loss of love, Anita disappears from their lives, refusing to become a competitor with her mother, but elated by the "exultant feeling of mastering herself, of plying herself to a difficult ideal, such as her Mother despised" (104). It is this daughter's loathing of her mother's self-centered, hedonistic lifestyle that is the guiding force which helps her determine her own values and approach to life quite apart from her mother.

81. Oates, Joyce Carol. "Matter and Energy." The Wheel of Love and Other Stories. New York: Vanguard Press, 1970. 334 – 361.

The movement of this story leaps back and forth in time over a 13-year period, tracing the disintegration of a mother-daughter relationship, strained by the mother's increasing mental instability. Although the narrator's mother remains hospitalized after her attempted suicide, she is still a compelling force in her daughter's life. "There are secrets in her she must tell me someday," the narrator writes. "I want to ask her, Why did you go crazy? I want to ask her, Why did you marry my father? I want to ask her, Why don't you let me go? Inside her skull, with its patchy gray hair, are all these secrets" (347).

As a child the daughter suffered from neglect and trauma when she discovered her mother trying to commit suicide. As an adult she is still haunted by the recurring memory of her deranged mother following the suicide attempt: "She has a face someone has clawed at, her hair is wild, streaked with blood; oh, her hands are the roots of trees torn out of the earth, and she longs to get back into that dark, dark air and that silence" (343). The daughter tries to maintain a tenuous relationship with her mother who suffers from paranoia and anxiety, feeling threatened yet exhilarated by her daughter's routine visits. The mother-daughter relationship described in this story has dissolved into an awkward bond based upon a need that neither mother nor daughter can understand or explain, for whatever feelings once existed between mother and daughter have been distorted by the shadow of mental illness.

82. Oates, Joyce Carol. "Shopping." Heat. New York: Dutton, 1991. 64 – 68.

The emotional estrangement of a middle-aged mother from her adolescent daughter is epitomized in this story, the entire action of which takes place during a shopping excursion. The mother loves her daughter "with a fierce unreasoned passion stronger than any she felt for the man who had been her husband for thirteen years, certainly far stronger than any she ever felt for her own mother" (56). But her daughter has drifted away into a self-absorbed world characteristic of many teenagers, alienating herself from her mother to the extent that her mother admits she no longer knows her own daughter. During the stopping trip, the mother hopes that together amid the crowds of shoppers, she and her daughter will discover "moments of intimacy" that are rarely possible when they are at home" (64). But the effort proves exhausting for both the mother and daughter who can no longer communicate or find common ground.

83. Patton, Frances Gray. "Mothers and Daughters." Twenty-eight Stories. New York: Dodd, Mead, and Company, 1969. 188 – 204.

The mother and her 17-year-old daughter in this story drift apart when the daughter enters a developmental phase where she appreciates art and beauty for the first time and questions accepted values. Criticizing her mother as trite and too practical, Laura withdraws emotionally from her mother, accusing her of "living on the surface." Despite the fact that Emily feels rejected by her daughter's hostility, she too remembers when she was 17 years old and still passionate (if not romantically naive) about life. Although

Emily's memory of her own adolescence cannot change her daughter's self-willed alienation, it does help this mother to understand and tolerate her daughter's remoteness as well as bear the pain of her maternal isolation.

84. Payne, Lucile Vaughn. "The Alien." The Boy Upstairs and Other Stories. New York: Follett, 1965. 61 – 76.

The mother in this story develops serious self-doubts about her ability to mother while she copes with the frustrations of raising a teenaged daughter. Only when she confides in another mother who voices similar frustrations in raising a teenaged daughter does she regain hope for her future relationship with her daughter. The first time Miranda openly admits to herself that her daughter has become a "monster" she is shocked at the thought that flies "unbidden out of some hidden cave in her mind." She tries to argue with herself by inventing rationalizations: "No, she isn't. She's just going through a phase. She's a teen-ager. She needs sympathy and understanding and patience. She's just oversensitive and proud and worried about being popular. Pressures are so awful on kids these days" (62). But the truth keeps surfacing: "She's a monster" (62). When the friction between mother and daughter reaches the point that Miranda feels tempted to strike her daughter in anger she has to admit, "I need help. I need a human voice to tell me what to do" (72). That help comes unexpectedly from the mother of her daughter's best friend who assures Miranda that she has experienced similar frustrations raising her own daughter. " 'I'll tell you something,' " Mrs. Gordon confesses to Miranda. " 'There are times when I'm not sure I can live through it' " (75). If all the other mothers of teenaged daughters appear to be calm and self-assured, they are wonderful actresses, Mrs. Gordon contends. " 'I've done some quiet investigating,' " she explains to Miranda. " 'All those women. Down underneath they're going mad. I mean it. You scratch any modern female with a teen-age daughter and you find a woman on the edge of hysterics. Believe me. It's the world's biggest secret society' " (75). The realization that she is not the only "alien" raising a typical teenaged daughter provides Miranda both comfort and hope for her sanity.

85. Portnoy, Marsha. "Loving Strangers." Family: Stories from the Interior. Ed. Geri Giebel Chavis. St. Paul: Graywolf Press, 1987. 93 – 100.

A mother and her adult daughter, who has recently given birth to her own daughter, attempt to become more than "loving strangers" during the casual visit which comprises the plot of this story. Although Marianne's mother seems to have both her house and life in perfect, enviable order, she admits past mistakes to her daughter during her visit and reveals herself as a human being capable of failure and disappointment. Marianne realizes she is but one of those disappointments:

> I know I am not the ideal daughter and my father has not turned out to be the knight in shining armor she may have dreamed of marrying. Who knows how many other failed dreams and broken promises she has collected, stored like the royal Doulton teacups she has locked away in the Sheraton cabinets? I think back and wonder how much sadness she has managed to conceal inside her beautiful, beautiful house. (99).

This daughter's insight into the carefully concealed side of her mother's character helps to humanize her mother as a woman capable of imperfection and equally capable of becoming more than a distant, "loving stranger" to both her daughter and granddaughter.

86. Potter, Nancy. "Safe Home." Legacies. Chicago: University of Illinois Press, 1987. 102 – 113.

This story traces the ill-fated life of an illegitimate daughter whose life is a series of failures until her death. From the beginning Jo, the product of a broken marriage, was a ruthless crier. Her mother "marked the days by the number of aspirin and whether Jo was a bad or worse than the day before. As soon as she could walk, she tried running away" (104). As Jo grew, different psychiatrists recommended a variety of approaches to her mother for managing her daughter's behavior, but none seemed to work. Jo grew up unmotivated, rebellious, and distant. When she bought a bus ticket to Colorado with no definite plan in mind, her mother heard from her only when she was in need of money. At the same time Becky became less of a mother to her faraway daughter, she became more of a mother to her own aging parents whose health began to fail. "Carrying trays into her parents' sickrooms and changing their beds, Becky felt that she had become their mother. Sending money to Jo to repair an ancient house or to have a well dug, she felt that she was supporting a sour pioneer grandmother" (107). After a silence of more than six months from her daughter, Becky was called one night to a hospital in a small southern city where her daughter, who has become a member of a religious cult, lay dying. Burying her daughter, Becky realized, was the most humane gift she could offer, for Jo was finally "safe home." In this story Potter portrays the tragedy of a mother-daughter connection that was never made and the sense of loss for a mother who outlives her daughter, and is subsequently left with only a series of joyless remembrances of her daughter's short life.

87. Randal, Vera. "Waiting for Jim." The Best American Short Stories 1964. Boston: Houghton Mifflin, 1964. 285 – 297.

An adolescent daughter on the verge of womanhood experiences a strong yearning for independence and sexual maturity while she feels an equally strong need to remain a child under the protection of her mother in this story. At the same time Nancy resents her mother's inability to recognize her merging sexuality and prepare her for womanhood, her behavior indicates she is still a child in emotional maturity in need of mothering. The rough and often painful transformation from childhood to womanhood and its impact on both mothers and daughters is illustrated in this narrative.

88. Robinson, Roxanna. "The Time for Kissing." A Glimpse of Scarlet and Other Stories. New York: Edward Burlingame Books, 1991. 9 – 28.

The narrator of this story, one of four children, describes her gradual estrangement from her mother who finalizes their physical and emotional distancing at the age of 71 when she announces in the midst of an awkward hug with her daughter that she is no longer kissing people. " 'I've never liked it,' " she admits to her daughter. " 'Harry's dead, and I don't have to kiss anyone now. I don't have to and so I don't. My time for kissing is over,' " (27). Crying in the presence of her mother for the first time that she can remember, the narrator weeps for all the intimate mother-daughter conversations they will never have because a mother who cannot kiss is a mother who will never be able to share experiences and emotions with her daughter; she is a woman truly alone.

89. Sanford, Annette. "Trip in a Summer Dress." Lasting Attachments. Dallas: Southern Methodist University Press, 1989. 57 – 70.

"If I was my mother," the daughter-narrator of this story writes, "I'd get mighty tired of always being right" (70). As the narrator leaves home at the age of 20 to marry a barbershop owner, her five-year-old son unaware that she is his mother and not his sister, she feels emotionally torn between motherhood and marriage. If she accepts her mother's advice, she can begin a new life free of maternal responsibilities, assured that her son will be raised and nurtured by his grandmother, whom he will always assume is his own mother. But if she follows her mother's advice, she will sacrifice truth and her own motherhood. Her other alternative is to confess the truth to her son and her betrothed for the first time, hopeful that neither will reject her as mother or wife. But this choice will undoubtedly be met with disapproval by her mother, who is invariably right most of the time.

While she was 15 years old and pregnant with Matthew, the narrator allowed her mother to assume the role of Matthew's mother while she begrudgingly complied with her mother's wishes and pretended to be his sister. "I got used to it," the narrator writes, "the way you do a thorn that won't come or chronic appendicitis. But it's hard to pretend all the time that something's true when it isn't," she confides. And it is hard to leave a child behind, knowing you will miss his sixth birthday and maybe his seventh as well, even if you do know your mother is right. It does not ease the pain of motherhood.

90. Sasaki, R. A. "Seattle." The Loom and Other Stories. St. Paul: Graywolf Press, 1991. 107 – 112.

The cultural values of a Japanese-American mother and her daughter conflict in this story, as the mother clings to Japanese traditions while the daughter identifies with more modern American values. When the narrator's father dies, the most natural consequence "from a Japanese standpoint" for a divorced daughter over thirty years of age would be for the daughter to move in with her widowed mother. "But I am not Japanese," the narrator asserts to herself as she defends her decision to continue to live alone:

> Perhaps I've just seen too many American movies. In American movies getting everything you want constitutes a happy ending. A satisfying Japanese ending, in contrast, has to have an element of sadness. There must be suffering and sacrifice—for these are proof of love. (108)

To the narrator's mother, the ideal mother-daughter relationship is one in which "invisible wires" unite mother and daughter in a "bond of obligation, of suffering, of love" (112). But her Americanized daughter rejects the traditional Japanese notions of suffering and sacrifice, becoming a less than ideal daughter who cannot speak her thoughts frankly with her mother, lest she risk offense.

91. Schutt, Christine. "These Women." The Pushcart Prize. IV: Best of the Small Presses. Ed. Bill Henderson. Yonkers: The Pushcart Press, 1979. 473 – 485.

"These Women" relates the experience of two young daughters, told from the perspective of the older daughter, who grow up with the social stigma of having a mother who is both divorced and mentally ill. The daughters are reared primarily by their maternal grandmother with only occasional trips to a sanitarium to visit their estranged mother, too self-absorbed in her own problems to handle the responsibilities of motherhood. The perception of her daughter the grandmother passes on to her granddaughters is one of disappointment and failure. " 'You're just like your mother,' " the grandmother taunts her granddaughter when she is especially disapproving. "When I have failed in math or morals," the narrator writes, "I am like my mother" (473). The two daughters in this story grow up deprived of the mother-daughter bond which their grandmother cannot provide. They are envious and at times resentful of other daughters whose mothers are emotionally supportive and always close by for them, not alienated and distracted as their own faraway mother.

92. Schwartz, Sheila. "Passover." Imagine a Great White Light. Wainscott, NY: Pushcart Press, 1991. 235 – 287.

The Jewish mother and her adult daughter in this story conflict when the mother attempts to control her daughter's life, continually "matchmaking, working out solutions for Shira's life," even after she enters college (268). The mother's assault upon her daughter's lifestyle, her future plans, and her devotion is so relentless that her daughter begins to have nightmares and even contemplates suicide as a way to join her ancestors who preceded her in death—ancestors who, unlike her mother, she envisions lovingly accepting her without judgment or reservation:

> All she has to do is leap through the water to the other side, through the hedge, to the dark canal, and she'll be there; they told her so. They're waiting for her there. All she has to do is leap; all waiting with arms outstretched across the stiffened grass.
>
> It's true. She only has to jump and she'll be there, across the canal where it's quiet and she can rest. No one will ask her questions there. No one will accuse her. They will welcome her with open arms. (283 – 284)

The alienation Shira feels is neither her fault nor her mother's, but simply "the way things are." She blames neither her mother nor herself for their alienation. However, so distanced are the two of them that Shira cannot find the words even to express this simple conclusion to her grieving mother.

93. Seagull, Thyme S. "My Mother Was a Light Housekeeper." The Woman Who Lost Her Names. Ed. Julia Wolf Mazow. New York: Harper and Row, 1980. 177 – 191.

An adult daughter tries to reconcile her lesbianism with her skeptical Jewish parents in this story. She confides to her mother that she felt isolated growing up with her secret, "trapped in the attic, like a bird," writing things she would admit to no one. Now she seeks her own identity and culture, a "native land" where she imagines herself as a part of an all-female tribe who will shout "Kinswoman!" to each other in a tribal tongue. Although her mother criticizes her daughter for living in a fantasy world removed from reality, regrets her daughter's change of name, and fears that her unconventional appearance may endanger her safety, she accepts her daughter's nontraditional life choices and remains supportive, a "Virgo woman, steadiness and continuation in seas of change" (191).

94. Sears, Vickie L. "Keeping Sacred Secrets." The Things That Divide Us. Eds. Faith Conlon, Rachel da Silva, and Barbara Wilson. Seattle: Seal Press, 1985. 45 – 61.

The mother and daughter in this story are divided by cultural differences which cannot be reconciled. Mary Ann is raised by her Native American father until his death necessitates her moving in with her Anglo mother, who insists that she abandon the Native American traditions of her father's family. " 'But I won't be what you want me to be,' " Mary Ann protests to her mother. " 'I'm already me' " (53). Despite the disapproval of her mother and the prejudices of the Anglo children who mistreat Mary Ann at school, she secretly clings to her native heritage while her mother nourishes the illusion that she is raising a "normal" daughter who will easily adapt to the ways of the Anglo world and find acceptance readily in an all-white Society.

95. Simpson, Mona. "You Leave Them." The Paris Review Anthology. Ed. George Plimpton. NewYork: W. W. Norton, 1990. 531 – 540.

A mother and her 12-year-old daughter grow closer during a road trip across the country in this story as the mother begins to recognizes that her daughter is no longer a child. The distinction between adult and child, often a source of conflict as the daughter asserts her independence while her mother continues to maintain her maternal authority, begins to dissolve as each one recognizes their years of living together are limited. At times the six more years the daughter must endure until she moves away from her mother seem endlessly stifling; at times it seems like the years are passing all too quickly. While each individual sometimes feels embarrassed that she does not measure up to the other's expectations as a mother or daughter, there is a bond of closeness that sustains their relationship through the inevitable conflicts of adolescence.

96. Slesinger, Tess. "Mother to Dinner." Between Mothers and Daughters: Stories Across a Generation. Ed. Susan Koppelman. New York: The Feminist Press at the City University of New York, 1985. 141 – 160.

The introduction to this narrative describes it as a story "about how daughters love, honor, fear, hide from, and long for their mothers—and how that mother-daughter knot is invisible to men" (142). The protagonist, a wife of less than a year, is torn between her emotions toward her mother, whom she feels she has abandoned by marrying, "reducing her to a stranger," and her equally intense feelings for her husband. With only the duties of a lonely housewife to fill the hours of each day, Katherine longs for the intimate conversations and closeness she once shared with her mother before her marriage. Yet she needs her husband's strength and rational decisiveness to fulfill her life as well. Because these two people obviously despise one another, Katherine feels like a "human shuttle" weaving her way back and forth from one to another, "the two opposites who supported her web" (149). Vacillating between the two people who mean the most in her life, Katherine feels free to be neither daughter nor wife but is trapped somewhere in between in a confused miasma of disappointment and depression, "unable to decide whether to swim backward or forward, tempted almost to close her eyes and quietly drown where she was" (154).

A thunderstorm which approaches during the afternoon the story takes place reminds Katherine of her own unsettling predicament. "She was surrounded, she could not escape. She was suspended, she could take refuge with neither Gerald nor her mother, she was caught fairly by the thunder . . . " (156). As the brunt of the storm shakes the house and malicious streaks of lightning splinter across the sky, Katherine panics in an attempt to escape its brutal force. But the storm only draws closer, even as it seems to enter her own body:

> Now everything was the storm. The storm, which had circled about the room, wished for closer nucleus, and entered her body. The lightning pierced her stomach, the thunder shook her limbs, and retreated, growling, to its home in her bowels. There was no escape for her: she was no longer imprisoned in the storm: the storm was imprisoned in her. (169)

Each clap of thunder demands of Katherine that a decision has to be made. Should she be a daughter to her mother? Or should she be a wife to Gerald? There is no way she can be both and not alienate the other. When the sound of the doorbell ringing breaks the intensity of the storm, Katherine wonders if the person at the door is her mother of her husband Whom does she want it to be? "She did not know. She knew only, as she closed her eyes and slowly turned the handle of the door, and drew it in toward herself, that she wished that one of them, Gerald or her mother, were dead" (160).

This story illustrates the stressful intensity of the dilemma of a daughter trapped between competing roles and needs, forced into a situation where, unable to reconcile the two, she must make a choice between her relationship with her mother or her husband.

97. Spivack, Kathleen. "Generations." The Honeymoon. Saint Paul: Graywolf Press, 1986. 37 – 43.

A daughter's perception of her mother changes in this story when she becomes a mother herself for the first time. Jan's mother has always been so neat and trim, so poised and in control, that Jan cannot believe that she ever suffered the pain of childbirth. During her mother's first visit as a new grandmother, Jan wonders: "Could this woman, this stranger, with whom Jan had lived and struggled most of her life, ever have cried out in pain or lost composure? Jan couldn't imagine it; her mother had always been so perfect, so organized. Jan was a poor, an inferior model" (40). Jan remains critical of her mother's lack of maternal warmth and resists her offers of assistance with the baby until she hears her newborn son and her mother playfully interacting.

For the first time since giving birth Jan allows herself to sleep, unworried, as she surrenders her reservations about her mother's maternal instincts as she shares the joys of caring for her first child.

98. Straayer, Arny Christine. "High Heels." Between Mothers and Daughters: Stories Across a Generation. Ed. Susan Koppelman. New York: The Feminist Press at the City University of New York, 1985. 279 – 284.

A mother and her adolescent daughter are reunited in this story of attempted reconciliation and understanding after a period of alienation and separation. The mother, who committed her daughter to a psychiatric hospital because she has become so unmanageable, feels awkward and remorseful in her daughter's presence after her release. She is fearful of rejection, while her daughter feels equally awkward and unworthy of her mother's love because she has not met her mother's expectations. Shy and tentative in each other's company, mother and daughter rely upon past memories of happier times as a starting point to healing their relationship and renewing their severed mother-daughter bond.

99. Susco, Carroll. "Sinking." Short Fiction By Women. 3.1 (1992): 83 – 86.

Building upon the image of the aging, gnarled feet of a mother criticized by her daughter while the two of them are sunning at the beach, this story explores the friction which distances a mother and her daughter as they search for flaws in one another's appearances. In both what is said and left unsaid between the two characters in this story Susco creates a strong sense of alienation that has come between mother and daughter. In the afterword to the story, Susco explains that "Sinking" is "more metaphoric and image-based than most of my other stories, perhaps because I can't discuss this type of relationship in a simple straightforward way because it's so emotionally charged for me" (86).

100. Tan, Amy. "Rules of the Game." American Voices: Best Short Fiction by Contemporary Authors. Ed. Sally Arteseros. New York: Hyperion, 1992. 155 – 167.

In this narrative a Chinese-American daughter exerts her independence and rejects the controlling influence her mother insists on maintaining over her life. The story originally began as a "cerebral piece about chess," Tan explains in the preface of the story, but then veered "to one that concerned the relationship between a girl and her greatest ally and adversary, her mother" (155). The daughter-narrator of the story learns to play chess at the age of six and refines her skill until at the age of nine she becomes a national chess champion, her mother continually pressuring her to improve her performance. Once her daughter has achieved fame, the mother insists on introducing her to everyone, to her embarrassment. Finally the daughter dares to confront her mother with the truth: " 'Why do you have to use me to show off? If you want to show off, then why don't you learn to play chess?' " (166). As her mother's eyes turn into "dangerous black slits" and her voice into "sharp silence," the daughter "runs until it hurts," no clear destination in mind, until she wanders back home hours later. Her mother neither admonishes nor punishes her, but simply denies her presence. " 'We not concerning with girl. This girl not have concerning for us' " (167). In the privacy of her own room the daughter imagines herself locked in a chess battle with "two angry black slits" for an opponent. As her opponent's black men overtake her own white pieces, the narrator imagines herself escaping as she feels her body growing lighter. She writes: "I rose up into the air and flew out the window. Higher and higher, above the alley, over the tops of tiled roofs, where I was gathered up by the wind and pushed up toward the night sky until everything below me disappeared and I was alone" (167).

101. Thomas, Maria. "The Visit." African Visas: A Novella and Stories. New York: Soho Press, 1991. 165 – 186.

Alienation between an adult daughter and her mother develops in this story when the daughter moves to Africa and assimilates into a different culture which her mother can neither understand nor appreciate. To the dismay of Mrs. Dubois, Beverly not only adjusts to Nigerian customs and traditions, but appreciates its art and culture as well, even naming her first son Adedayo (whom Mrs. Dubois secretly calls David). But to Mrs. Dubois, the crude and often unsanitary living conditions of most Nigerians is insulting to her upbringing; it is painful for her to discover during her first visit that her daughter has fit so comfortably into such a uncivilized existence. " 'I am sure, Beverly,' " she confides to her daughter, " 'that our ancestors came from some other part of Africa. A nicer part' " (177). Surely the primitive artwork she finds displayed in her daughter's living room was "meant to be hidden in museums and looked at only by anthropologists who had perspective. Not kept alive in people's home or in their minds" (178). Once back in the United States, Mrs. Dubois serves tea, gingersnaps, and exotic tales of Africa to her engrossed friends, glossing over details of her daughter's life to avoid embarrassment, and resolves never to return to Africa, even if it means never seeing her daughter again.

102. Volk, Patricia. "Come Fly With Me." All It Takes. New York: Atheneum, 1990. 195 – 205.

This narrative explores the concept of "distancing" in mother-daughter relationships. "Distancing" has become the favorite topic of the narrator's mother characterized in this story, especially during her daughter's increasingly infrequent visits home. To the mother, distancing represents the erosion of a once close relationship based upon need. Her daughter, she realizes now, does not confide in her anymore and finds excuses to visit less frequently. When mother and daughter are together, their conversations are marked by extreme politeness instead of genuine feelings.

Although she denies the truth to her mother in order to spare her feelings, the daughter-narrator of the story is gradually and voluntarily distancing herself from a mother she neither admires nor feels she needs anymore.

103. Volk, Patricia. "My Mother's Kiss." All It Takes. New York: Atheneum, 1990. 125 – 133.

The dynamics of triangulated mother-daughter relationships are explored in this story. The narrator admits that she and her mother and sister are "never all on speaking terms at the same time." She explains: "When my mother is angry at Sukey, she talks to Sukey through me. When my mother is angry at me, as she seems to be now, she talks to me through Sukey. Between us, we have explored every mathematical permutation of the number three. When who talks to whom, it means whom is not talking to whomever" (125). In response for her mother's refusal to express her anger, the narrator plans to turn down her mother's offer to throw a party for her fortieth birthday, lying politely that she could never narrow down her list of extensive friendships to her mother's suggested limitation of six. She and her mother will fondly kiss and say good-bye, leaving the narrator with a sense of incompleteness and "a smell that's sweet and sour, flowery and dank, cool and warm, clean and dusty, fleshy and artificial" that will linger long after her mother is gone (132 – 133).

104. Walker, Alice. "Everyday Use." Close Company: Stories of Mothers and Daughters. Eds. Christine Park and Caroline Heaton. New York: Ticknor and Fields, 1989. 133 – 142.

The attitudes of two black daughters toward life are contrasted in this story. While the introverted daughter clings to the traditional, simple life her mother has always led, the extroverted one dismisses the traditional ways of her family as antiquated, glorifies her image while she changes her name, and sets out to improve the future of her race. "You ought to try to make something of yourself," she advises her sister. "It's really a new day for us. But from the way you and Mama still live you'd never know it" (140). But her words of advice and flamboyant lifestyle have little effect on her mother and daughter who are bonded in the pleasure of a peaceful lifestyle unhurried by the threat of change.

105. Walker, Alice. "How Did I Get Away with Killing One of the Biggest Lawyers in the State? It Was Easy." Ms. Nov. 1980. 72 – 75.

A black daughter narrates this story of tragedy and triumph in which a mother's life is sacrificed and a daughter gains revenge. The narrator, an illegitimate daughter, describes her childhood of poverty as a dependent of a mother who made $6 per day cleaning the homes of wealthy white folks. The daughter describes how she became a private prostitute for one of her mother's clients during her adolescence and with his help, had her mother committed to an insane asylum because she strongly disapproved of their relationship. But by the time the narrator begins to realize that her mother was right, her mother has become "as vacant as an empty eye socket" living in the asylum and dies before she has the chance to know her daughter has sought revenge and taken the life of the white lawyer who destroyed her relationship with her daughter. Issues of racial relations and adolescent need for acceptance alienate the mother and daughter in this story, who are never given the opportunity to reconcile their conflicting points of view before the mother's life is tragically cut short.

106. Walters, Anna Lee. "Apparitions." The Sun is Not Merciful. Ithaca: Firebrand Books, 1985. 83 – 90.

The Native American mother and daughter in this narrative are united in their collective alienation from the world of white Americans. During a shopping trip in a predominantly white town, Marie Horses and Wanda encounter hostility and racial prejudice from the white townspeople they meet. While a sales clerk ignores the soft-spoken request of Marie Horses, a shoe salesman sexually accosts Wanda. Both mother and daughter are treated as inferior and ignorant, but together they give each other strength to maintain their pride and self-respect. They both agree that coming to town is a chore to be endured, not enjoyed by mother and daughter.

107. Wilbur, Ellen. "Wealth." Wind and Birds and Human Voices. Winston-Salem: Stuart Wright, 1984. 35 – 44.

In this narrative a young daughter who uncharacteristically fails to inherit her wealthy mother's passion for acquiring materials goods is left with an intense longing for something missing in their relationship. In order to make up for her own deficient childhood, Esther's mother showers her daughters with possessions, even as she becomes addicted to materialism herself. Esther is the only daughter of three who confuses her mother by refusing to accept her repeated gifts, by seeming to desire so little for herself. " 'It isn't normal for a child not to want things,' " Esther's mother expresses her worries to her father (39). The only gift Esther really wants from her mother is her closeness and compatibility, intangibles which her mother has hopelessly confused with mother-daughter shopping sprees and mutual thirst for more possessions and higher social status.

108. Yamamoto, Hisaye. "Seventeen Syllables." Between Mothers and Daughters: Stories Across a Generation. Ed. Susan Kopelman. New York: The Feminist Press at the City University of New York, 1985. 161 – 176.

An adolescent daughter's emerging sexuality is contrasted with her Japanese-American mother's dim view of marriage in this story. Miserable in her own marriage of convenience which enabled her to emigrate to the United States and oppressed by a husband who shows little compassion for her feelings or respect for her artistic talents, Rosie's mother begs her daughter to promise never to marry, hoping to spare her daughter a similar agony. But Rosie has just experienced her first tentative, sexual encounter with a male, an awakening of great curiosity and pleasure. To respond to her mother's plea at such a time in her life would be to deny those feelings which have emerged for the first time. Neither daughter nor mother admits their unspoken differences of opinion out of respect for one another, but each feels the grief of her inability to share similar feelings.

Sources:

Stolp, Diane E. "Briefly Noted." Rev. of A Glimpse of Scarlet, by Roxanna Robinson. Belles Lettres. Spring, 1992: 59.

4

Death

INTRODUCTION

In the introduction to Loss of the Ground-Note: Women Writing About the Loss of Their Mothers, Helen Vozenilek describes the mother-daughter relationship as "one of the most charged, complex and crucial relationships women will ever have." Although some women "begin exploring this dynamic" while their mothers are still alive, Vozenilek explains, others begin a "deeper search and scrutiny" only after their mothers have died (8).

Karen Kandik writes of her surprise at finding herself still alive following the death of her mother in her essay "Finding Home":

> Not long after my mother died I realized I was surprised that I was still alive and had not died with her. It was not that I had ever consciously thought that I would die if my mother did: I had just never thought of life without her. (166)

The short stories in this chapter force us to imagine life without our mothers. The loss expressed by many motherless daughters is both "unique and universal," separate yet similar, writes Vozenilek. "Writing is but one medium through which women explore and share the experience of being motherless" (8). The majority of women who have authored the short stories included in this chapter examine the impact of death upon daughters who are left motherless; a minority of these writers reverse the expected sequence of death and examine the impact of daughters' untimely deaths upon their mothers.

Death is the final stage of separation between mother and daughter. Even after mothers die, however, their influences continue to impact the lives of their daughters, these stories tell us. The daughter in Hortense Calisher's "The Middle Drawer" begins to realize the intensity of this influence when she unlocks the contents of her mother's forbidden desk drawer shortly after her death. The continuing presence of a deceased Jewish mother is felt equally strongly by a single daughter in Aviva Cantor's "The Phantom Child" who is trying to decide whether or not to have an abortion. Although many factors weigh in her decision, it is the voice of her mother and her own continuing reevaluation of their relationship which influences her decision the most.

Daughters in short narratives written by Elizabeth Cook-Lynn, Misha Gallagher, and Ursula K. Le Guin regret the timing of their mothers' deaths before they have an opportunity to reconcile differences with their mothers. The Native-American daughter in Cook-Lynn's "Flight" is filled with regrets as she is en route to her mother's bedside, not knowing if her flight will arrive in time to allow her to see her mother alive. As she thinks of the many things she did and failed to do as a daughter, she feels overcome with an urgency to reestablish a relationship with her mother before it is too late. The lesbian daughter in Misha Gallagher's "Stories Don't Have Endings" regrets her mother's inability to accept her sexual identity and looks upon her relationship with her mother as an "unfinished dialogue" of unspoken emotions and unreconciled conflict. The adult daughter in Ursula K. Le Guin's "Crosswords" invokes the memory of her deceased mother as best she can, "trying to listen to what I didn't hear" while her mother was still alive.

It is only after her mother's death that the daughter in Kate Braverman's "Squandering the Blue" begins to realize that her mother did love her as a child and sacrificed the freedom of movement that provided the impetus to her writing talent to give her daughter a sense of stability in her life. Although the daughter-narrator cannot reverse time and revise her relationship with her mother, she can recognize and nurture the part of her she has inherited from her mother: "I know that whatever is excitable and open in me," she writes, "all that desires magnitude and grace, this is her legacy" (16). Similarly, it takes the death of the aging grandmother in Willa Cather's "Old Mrs. Harris" for her daughter and granddaughter to be startled out of their own self-centeredness and begin to appreciate the mother who has permanently disappeared from their lives.

Several of these stories examine the last days that mothers and daughters spend together before death separates them permanently. Mothers and daughters in Jayne Anne Phillips's "Souvenirs" and Lois F. Lyles's "Last Christmas Gift From a Mother" openly share their intimate thoughts about death with one another—thoughts they refuse to share with anyone else—while the mother and daughter in Stephanie Vaughn's "My Mother Breathing Light" never openly discuss "the secret that each of us keep from each other."

The daughter in Moira Crone's "Crocheting" crochets a cap for her mother's head, balded by chemotherapy treatments, as a parting gift. She envisions the cap keeping her mother's head warm and her sanity intact until she soon succumbs to cancer. Deena Linett's "Gifts" explores the feelings of a daughter who helps her father prepare her mother's dead body for burial as "the last act of loving kindness" they can offer her together. "I had never seen anyone who was dead before," she admits her feelings of anxiety and self-doubt. "I was stunned and terrified that I would scream, or cry; fail him and her" (71). In contrast, the daughter in Nancy Roberts's "A Proper Introduction" admits she avoided her mother during the last few months of her life because she feared that witnessing her mother's deteriorating condition would make her weaker and more vulnerable. She writes, following the death of her mother:

> It was as if my visits to my mother tore off a layer that kept me from feeling the world's dangers—or from a great rage and sorrow endangering from within. Uncovered, too, was the worry that I didn't really love her, not enough anyhow to stop avoiding her. Yet mother had approved in her way. When I was "myself," I was competent, everyone said, talented, and even independent. "You're the strong

> one in the family," she used to tell me. To remain so, I had avoided her. (48)

The daughter in Alice Ryerson's semi-autobiographical narrative "Do Not Disturb" honors her mother's wish by not interfering when her mother decides it is time to end her own life. When that moment arrives, the narrator does not try to persuade her mother to change her mind, for that would violate her wish. Yet the daughter-narrator cannot bear to stay with her mother during the suicidal act, even though she realizes that her mother would appreciate her presence and support. In "What is Seized" Lorrie Moore points out that it is the memory of the last night a mother and daughter spend together that etches itself indelibly in the daughter's mind. She writes:

> Once they die, of course, you get the strand of pearls, the blue quilt, some of the original wedding gifts—a tray shellacked with the invitation, an old rusted toaster—but the touches and the words and the moaning the night she dies, these are what you seize, save, carry around in little invisible envelopes, opening them up quickly, like a carnival huckster, giving the world a peek. They will not stay quiet. No matter how you try, No matter how you lick them. The envelopes will not stay glued. (39 – 40)

The mother in Lois F. Lyles's "Last Christmas Gift From a Mother" offers her daughter a parting gift—an opportunity to witness death as a test of her personal strength. During childhood, the daughter-narrator recalls, her parents made sure that all of her needs were met and that she was "never exposed to the sight of physical suffering." "But an easy ride of a life is only a half-truth," she now realizes. "Now Mama's gift is to let me know her pain. She is letting me see if I am strong enough to grapple, by proxy, with Death" (247). The aging mother who narrates Anna Tuttle Villegas's "Do Not Go Gentle" realizes that with her death, her daughter will gain something valuable as she begins a new phase of "final growth, the setting-in of the poise and grace of maturity" (23).

Molly Giles uses the death of a mother to illustrate the differences that have prevented closeness between a mother and daughter in "Rough Translations." While Romana, a free-spirited artist, envisions her idyllic funeral as a nontraditional celebration of wine, music, and witty conversation performed on the side of a mountain slope with herself hovering in the clouds above "like a Chagall bride," she knows that her daughter will plan a much more traditional ceremony with too many flowers and piped-in Muzak for the proper mourning of a mother she has never really loved.

Tina Marie Conway's "World War II Picture" stands as a tribute to a mother whose image is preserved indefinitely in a World War Two photograph as a warm and passionate, strong and supportive woman. This image serves to balance the one her daughter will never be able to forget of a frail woman fighting a losing battle with cancer at the age of 57. The daughter in Marilyn Krysl's "Looking For Mother," however, has neither memories nor photographs to remember her mother, who died as she was giving birth to her daughter. Now the adult daughter has only her imagination to fantasize a series of maternal images as she tries to piece together a composite of the mother she has never known. Similarly, the daughter in Laura Marello's "Catch Me Go Looking" tries to piece together sketchy details and distant memories to recreate a lasting impression of her mother who committed suicide when she was still a child.

In stories written by Susan Engberg, Cynthia Ozick, Jane Yolen, Sallie Bingham, and Rachel Simon, daughters precede their mothers in death. Susan Engberg's "Pastorale" describes the phases of a mother's grief who loses her daughter at the age of ten. In Cynthia Ozick's "The Shawl" a horrified concentration camp prisoner witnesses the brutal beating of her infant daughter by the guard who discovers her carefully concealed existence. The 13-year-old daughter in Jane Yolen's "Names" gradually starves herself as a self-sacrifice for her mother who continually recites the names of Holocaust victims, lest their memory be forgotten. A drug-dealing mother murders her own 14-year-old daughter in Rachel Simon's "The Greatest Mystery of Them All." The daughter-narrator, who now resides in heaven, watches her mother below as she awaits her arrival so that she can "finally give her a piece of my mind" (51).

Mothers in stories written by Karen Brennan, Laura Marello, Amy Hempel, Alice Ryerson, and Elizabeth Spencer commit suicide, often before their daughters have the opportunity to build strong mother-daughter relationships. While the majority of these mothers end their lives for personal reasons or because of mental instability, the aging mother in Spencer's "First Dark" commits suicide in order to give her daughter the freedom to marry. Knowing that her daughter is torn between her need for constant care and her own desire to become a wife, Mrs. Harvey executes a carefully planned suicide in order to release her daughter from the bondage of her care.

Although death may separate mothers and daughters, the bond between them remains always, these short stories remind us. Many daughters would undoubtedly agree with Alison Townsend who writes in her essay "Small Comforts." that her mother, who died of breast cancer when Alison was nine years old, remains "both with me and not with me, alive and gone." Townsend describes how her mother's continued presence has shaped—and even haunted—her life even into adulthood. She writes:

> I am forever different from my women friends who still have their mothers. I am not the same woman I would have been if she'd lived. And I did not, after the age of nine, have the same girlhood. But as to whether either would have been better or worse, I cannot say. All I can say with certainty is that I am haunted by her. That there is a rent, a tear, a rip in the fabric of my life that can't ever be completely sewn up or patched over, but which lets in both the darkness that is the underworld and a world of astonishing—the only word which can describe it is celestial—light. That my mother is both with me and not with me, alive and gone. And, that though these words begin to tell some small part of the story, it is a story, I will probably be telling all my life—of a girl and her mother and the love which connects them, like a strong rope, or an umbilical cord, running faithfully between this world and whatever world comes next. (122)

SHORT FICTION

109. Ackerman, Felicia. "The Forecasting Game: A Story." Prize Stories 1990: The O.Henry Awards. Ed. William Abrahams. New York: Doubleday, 1990. 315 – 335.

The author of this award-winning narrative parallels the prediction of her mother's death with the forecasting of weather in a story of love and disappointment. Hospitalized with leukemia but preferring the state of dying to death itself, Charlotte's aging but dauntless mother agrees to undergo an experimental treatment and begins to show improvement, only to suddenly die. Charlotte, a philosophy professor and meteorology student, senses parallels in her own emotions toward her mother's death and the variability of weather patterns, feeling "too desolate to cry" immediately after her mother dies just as it can be "too cold to snow" outside (333). Predicting longevity and forecasting weather are both games, Charlotte realizes, played with uncertainty and much caution. Not all forecasts do come true, and no one lives in an insulated bubble protected from the snowstorm.

110. Bingham, Sallie. "Pleyben." New Stories by Southern Women. Ed. Mary Ellis Gibson. Columbia: University of South Carolina Press, 1989. 47 – 53.

This story contrasts the feelings and reactions of a mother and father toward their daughter six months after her death in a motorcycle accident. While the bereaved father remains numb and cannot begin to imagine the details of his daughter's existence anymore, his wife visualizes her daughter as a person continuing to grow even though she has been buried. " 'So now when I think of her,' " the mother tells her husband, " 'I think of the way her body is going on, underground, growing. . . . Her hair and fingernails, of course. But something else, too. The cells. I think the cells are growing down there in the damp. The skin cells and the ones underneath that would have turned into babies' " (51 – 52). With vivid imagery and detail, the mother recalls her daughter's life from birth through adolescence. Her husband envies his wife's imaginative capacity to remain close to her daughter in this special way and begs her to help him develop the same closeness. But the mother refuses, realizing that the images she has of her daughter, both past and present, are the result of the intimate relationship she shared with her daughter and are not skills that can be taught to someone else.

111. Braverman, Kate. "Squandering the Blue." Squandering the Blue. New York: Fawcett Columbine, 1990. 1 – 16.

This narrative compares the adverse feelings of a young daughter for her mother with her revised, more accepting feelings as an adult who only then recognizes that she was loved by her mother. As a child, the daughter resents her mother as a failure because she cannot provide her daughter with a father, a steady income, an acceptable role model, or a home of their own. "My mother can't even stay sober," the daughter complains. The mother's attempts to write poetry are looked upon by her daughter as "a dubious enterprise, an excuse for failing to live normally" (10). "The other mothers play tennis and bridge, they make dinner parties, attend premiers, and go on location. They are tanned and assured. They don't have gray hair. My mother is not like them at all. I don't care if she drinks vodka until she dies" (12).

When her mother dies of breast cancer, her daughter expresses a sense of relief that an embarrassing burden has been removed from her life. Death presents her with an opportunity to use sympathy for social mobility as she becomes the center of attention as the "only orphan in Westford Academy."

It is with the passage of time and deepening of understanding that comes with maturity that the impressions of her mother gradually change form. "I don't know precisely when I was first overtaken by these longings for her," the adult daughter now writes. "I cannot say when shame and cruelty were transformed into love, what secret bridges must be built or how much structures are devised and crossed. I am much older" (14). The narrator now realizes that when her mother stopped moving from one exotic place to another in order to provide her daughter with some sense of stability, she sacrificed the freedom that was the impetus for her writing. Although she cannot reverse time and revise her childhood antipathy toward her mother, the daughter-narrator can now recognize and nurture the part of her mother she has inherited: "I know that whatever is excitable and open in me, all that desires magnitude and grace, this is her legacy" (16).

112. Brennan, Karen. "C'est la Vie." Wild Desire. Amherst: University of Massachusetts Press, 1991. 27 – 34.

The daughter of a mentally disturbed woman in this story must cope with her mother's delusions of grandeur as well as her eventual suicide. Proclaiming herself a novelist, the mother quits her job as a shoe sales clerk to write full time and pursue her dream as a writer. But while Nadell is being fired from her job at a fast food restaurant for thwarting the advances of the manager, her mother quietly shoots herself. Nadell uses her imaginative powers to help her rise above the uncertainty and monotony that characterized her life with her mother. As she is falling asleep, Nadine has a "fleeting impression" of a gun exploding near her head and dreams she is on an airplane which has just exploded, bodies strewn everywhere in the aftermath. But somehow she manages to disentangle herself from the wreckage,"and since there was no gravity in this dream, she shot beautifully into the clouds" (33).

113. Broner, Esther Masserman (as E. M. Broner). "My Mother's Madness." Ms. July/Aug. 1991: 49 – 54.

This narrative focuses on the perceptions of a daughter who witnesses the gradual mental demise of her mother as she nears death. As her mother's mental acuity deteriorates, the narrator describes her as a woman who becomes more paranoid and delusionary, alternating between the present to the past 70 years ago when she witnessed the violent upheaval of society during the Russian Revolution and later emigrated to the United States. The aging mother often confuses the past and present in her mind, as she vaccilates between mental clarity and confusion. She imagines cossacks on the roof, the muzhiks stealing her possessions. Yet she realizes accurately when she purchases her medicine at the pharmacy that the cost has tripled. "They take advantage of the weak, the elderly, and the sick," she cries.

"It's become a nation of thieves" (52). The daughter who narrates this story characterizes her mother as a woman who never loses her wit or gift of verbal expression even as the illness which invades her body clouds and confuses her perception of reality.

114. Brown, Suzanne. "Communion." New Stories from the South: The Year's Best, 1986. Ed. Shannon Ravenel. Chapel Hill: Algonquin Books, 1986. 39–49.

The funeral of a grandmother brings together a mother and daughter for a brief communion of closeness before the circumstances of their lives separate them once more in this story. Although Gladys attempts to communicate with her mother during her visit, Mamie refuses to express her emotions openly or listen to the problems of her daughter who remains a casual stranger in her house. Mamie feels a greater closeness to the mother she has just buried than to her own daughter, whom she realizes will never experience the pleasure of washing and setting her dead mother's hair for burial, an act of love she has just performed for her own mother. The geographical and emotional distance between them is too great to expect such daughterly devotion.

115. Calisher, Hortense. "The Middle Drawer." The Collected Stories of Hortense Calisher. New York: Arbor House Publishing Company, Inc., 1975. 289–298.

The entire content of this narrative takes place in the mind of an adult daughter about to unlock her mother's drawer a week after she has succumbed to cancer. While Hester's mother was alive their relationship was strained by unresolved differences, complicated by each one's search for a warmth denied during Hester's childhood. In retrospect, turning the key in her hand as she contemplates opening the drawer, Hester realizes that while her mother was living, she was always searching for the "final barb, the homing shaft, that would maim her mother once and for all, as she felt herself to have been maimed," and cancer provided that fatal barb (296).

But death does not permit Hester to escape her mother's controlling hand. The memories contained within the middle drawer, Hester realizes as she begins to unlock its contents, are but reminders that death never absolves the living. The living carry, Hester concludes, "perhaps not one tangible wound but the burden of the innumerable small cicatrices imposed on us by our beginnings; we carry them with us always, and from these, from this agony, we are not absolved" (298). A mother's influence in her daughter's life continues on even after death severs the mother-daughter bond.

116. Cantor, Aviva. "The Phantom Child." The Woman Who Lost Her Names. Ed. Julia Wolf Mazow. New York: Harper and Row, 1980. 105–112.

A deceased Jewish mother in this story becomes a powerful presence in her childless daughter's life who, at age 31, must decide whether or not to have an abortion. While the narrator is torn between giving birth and having an abortion, feeling like like a "tortured laboratory animal in an impossible image" with two exits, both of which administer an electric shock, she hears the voice of her mother "exhorting, begging, pleading, threatening, inducing guilt: nagging" her to have this baby. Many questions weigh heavily in the narrator's decision, the most difficult of these originating from her relationship with her mother, which she fears she may repeat if she gives birth to her own child. She wonders:

> Do I want to have an abortion to spite my mother (even though she will never know)? Or do I want to have the baby to placate her? To diminish my guilt (it can never be removed) by doing something for her? To do this thing that I don't want to do as punishment for killing her so that I can stop punishing myself in other ways? (111)

If she has the abortion, the narrator realizes, she may be left alone in old age, "a shopping-bag lady on the streets of New York, a prey of muggers" (110). Although her own mother did give birth to a daughter, "that was as good as having none at all," she berates herself in her own mind. She remembers herself as an "insensitive and inconsiderate" daughter who failed to reconcile differences with her mother before she died and now is haunted by leftover guilt. Although there are many factors which affect her choice, it is her relationship with her mother which has the most influence upon the narrator's decision of whether or not to abort.

117. Cather, Willa. "Old Mrs. Harris." Obscure Destinies. New York: Alfred A. Knopf, 1932. 75 – 190.

Mrs. Harris, the aged, selfless mother and grandmother characterized in this novella, attempts to die unnoticed so as not to disrupt the life of her daughter and family. So self-absorbed in their own concerns are her family members that it is an easy task for Mrs. Harris to pass away without notice. While Mrs. Harris recognizes that she is experiencing her last few hours of life, her daughter is locked in her room, preoccupied with the devastating news that she is facing motherhood again even as her daughter is about to enter college, that she must endure another pregnancy that would surely make her "ill and hideous for months" once more. Only after the death of Mrs. Harris are the members of the household "startled out of their intense self-absorption." But by then it is too late. Cather predicts that only as Mrs. Harris's daughter and granddaughter begin to grow older and less self-centered will they grow closer to the mother and grandmother they have lost and perhaps find themselves dying alone and unnoticed as well. She writes:

> When they are old, they will come closer and closer to Grandma Harris. They will think a great deal about her, and remember things they never noticed; and their lot will be more or less like hers. They will regret that they heeded her so little; but they, too, will look into the eager, unseeing eyes of young people and feel themselves alone. They will say to themselves: "I was heartless, because I was young and strong and wanted things so much. But now I know." (190)

118. Conway, Tina Marie. "World War II Picture." The Luxury of Tears: Winning Stories from the National Society of Arts and Letters Competition. Little Rock: August House, 1989. 61 – 71.

This narrative is a daughter's tribute to her mother who faces a premature death at the age of 57. As the mother succumbs to cancer, her daughter carries with her a lasting impression of her mother as a vibrant young war wife embodied in a photograph sent to her husband overseas during World War Two. The mother she remembers as strong but warm before cancer invaded her body is also preserved in the photograph as a young woman of passion and playfulness with enough resemblance to her own daughter that they could have been mistaken for the same individual. This image of a woman—"ready to fight, to wait, to always be here"—captured by the camera's eye balances the final memory she retains of her mother as a frail woman succumbing to her own battle with death. The woman in the photograph is remembered and admired in her daughter's mind as both a mother and a woman prepared to confront whatever life presents her.

119. Cook-Lynn, Elizabeth. "Flight." The Power of Horses and Other Stories. New York: Little, Brown and Company, 1990. 90 – 93.

The Native American daughter who narrates this story expresses a sense of desperation as she is in flight to her mother's bedside, not knowing if she will arrive before her mother dies. For two years her aging mother has hovered near death, "rallying, weakening, resisting, and constantly asking someone for a way out" (90). Now, full of regrets for the many things she did and did not do as a daughter, the narrator feels overcome with a feeling of urgency to reestablish their relationship before her mother dies. "I just want her to look at me again and know that I came," she writes. "That's all. Just if she can see me. She will know me. . . . I want to tell her. . . . I want to tell her. . . " (92 – 93).

120. Crone, Moira. "Crocheting." American Made. Eds. Mark Leyner, Curtis White, and Thomas Glynn. New York: Fiction Collective, 1986. 55 – 60.

The daughter who narrates this story crochets a cap for her hospitalized mother as a parting gift, knowing that her mother will soon succumb to cancer. As chemotherapy treatments have robbed her mother of her hair, cancer has bloated her head into a swollen, gray balloon. The cap, the daughter imagines as she visits and continues to crochet, will serve to help keep her mother's head warm while it prevents ideas from escaping, lest her mother forget her own name and the identity of her own daughter, as the course of the cancer progresses.

121. Engberg, Susan. "Pastorale." Pastorale. Chicago: University of Illinois Press, 1982. 33 – 51.

This story seeks to describe the changing stages of grief and forms of sorrow in a mother's life as she continues the lifelong process of learning to accept the premature death of a daughter and reconcile that loss. When Hanna died at the age of ten, Catherine was 40. As the years pass, Catherine looks forward and backward in time, seeing nothing but "inexpressive decades" that now characterize her life.

> But beneath this methodical impassive continuance of life, she could feel her grief changing into something less bearable than the immediate anguish; it was a sense of absolute physical loss, of strange yearning: she wanted to touch the child again. There had been no chance to be alone with her, dead. At night Catherine would lie in the dark and think that she might be all right if only she could cradle the child's actual corpse one more time. (34)

Although Catherine's continuing roles of artist, wife, and mother of two adolescent sons occupy her time and attention, she continues to find her sorrow for the loss of her daughter evolving in phases as it assumes varied forms, which she "must simply wait and accept."

122. Floyd, Patty Lou. "When Mother Played Moonshine." The Silver Desoto. Tulsa: Council Oak Books, 1987. 69 – 97.

This narrative describes the sensitive impressions of an adolescent daughter during the last summer she spends with her mother, knowing that she will soon die. Each day is packed full of literature, philosophy, picnics, and intimate secrets. "All that summer," the narrator writes, "it was as though I were going off to make my way in life and she was packing everything I would need—a few social graces, a few friends, a few practical skills, a few windows onto beauty, and overall of these, a tonic dash of heresy" (85). During those last remaining months of her mother's life, "while the vines on the porch grew fuller and less lacy, while the baby jays left their next and their mother left off her fretting, I learned about comedy and tragedy, original sin and Darwin, pinking shears and French seams," the narrator remembers (86). One of the most important lessons of life she learned from her mother that summer was when to laugh and when to cry, and it is long after her mother's death that she finally allows the tears to come, "wracking and unquenchable" as she remembers the dramatic image of her mother as an amateur actress "playing Moonshine."

123. Gallagher, Misha. "Stories Don't Have Endings." Spider Woman's Granddaughters: Traditional Tales and Contemporary Writings by Native American Women. Ed. Paula Gunn Allen. Boston: Beacon Press, 1989. 221– 226.

The lesbian daughter who narrates this story expresses regrets that her mother died before they could reconcile their "years of intense struggle," struggle for "control on my mom's part, for autonomy on mine" (222). Although her mother knew she had a "butch daughter," the narrator writes, "she never openly accepted her daughter's sexual orientation, making it difficult for her daughter to express her real identity. Long after the death of the mother, the daughter feels a haunting sense of loss that her relationship with her mother remains an "unfinished dialogue" of unspoken emotion and unreconciled conflict. "I keep feeling," the daughter writes, "that I want to phone home and talk to her. That unfinished dialogue. A way to explain those things I hope she now knows" (226).

124. Gerber, Merrill Joan. "The Cost Depends on What You Reckon It In." Stop Here, My Friend. Boston: Houghton Mifflin, 1965. 15 – 31.

This narrative traces the gradual demise of an aging Jewish mother and her daughter's powerlessness to prevent her unhappiness and eventual death. Unable to care her for mother at home, the daughter reluctantly places her in a nursing home where her mother begins to lose her memory and her incentive to live. The daughter tries to assuage her own guilt by sneaking forbidden kosher food to her mother, but she refuses to eat, for fear the food might prolong a life she no longer wants to live. The daughter attempts to prevent her mother's death, but the medical neglect she has suffered in the nursing home has already taken its course. When her mother's body is almost mistakenly buried in the wrong grave, the daughter succeeds in postponing the burial one day so that her mother can be buried next to her husband, as planned. But in her minor victory the daughter earns the right to bury her mother alone, pitching a handful of dirt on the wooden coffin, as custom dictates, surrendering her mother to the earth in hopes that she will at last find peace.

125. Gilchrist, Ellen. "Indignities." In the Land of Dreamy Dreams. Fayetteville: University of Arkansas Press, 1981. 103 – 107.

An eccentric mother with breast cancer predicts her time of death and plans her funeral with her closest friends and daughter in this story. The daughter, from whose viewpoint the narrative is written, feels somehow deficient, convinced that surely she was a disappointment to her mother because her life has been so uneventful compared to her mother's—"no illicit drugs, no unwanted pregnancies, no lesbian affairs, no irate phone calls from teachers, never a moment's doubt that I was living up to my potential," she writes (104). She dutifully carries out her mother's last wishes, joining the chosen few who lower the casket into the grave and shovel dirt upon it, as she watches the last vestiges of her childhood disappear with the burial of her mother.

126. Giles, Molly. "Rough Translations." Rough Translations. Athens: University of Georgia Press, 1985. 120 – 135.

A mother's death in this story accentuates the differences between herself and her daughter which have prevented their developing a close relationship. A disheveled artist who panics at the thought of dying with so much unfinished work yet to be done, Ramona will not let herself die until she has planned each detail of her idyllic funeral. She fantasizes a nontraditional ceremony held on a mountain slope—a celebration of wine, music, and witty conversation where she is present herself, "hovering in the sky like a Chagall bride, her pretty shroud rippling around her crossed ankles" (126). In reality Ramona knows her funeral will not be such a joyous occasion. Under the direction of her daughter's crisp, efficient direction, her body will be draped in mauve with her fingernails and lips appropriately matched in color. The chapel will "smell unwholesomely floral," and Muzak will be piped in as Nora counts heads, wondering if she has made enough potato salad. She will tell the guests how Ramona became "dependent and docile" toward the end, as if she were the child and Nora became the mother. Dressed handsomely in black, Nora will mourn appropriately for the mother she never really loved, the unconventional mother who drew cartoons, lived as a free spirit, and loathed mauve.

127. Haardt, Sara. "Miss Rebecca." Southern Album. Ed. H. L. Mencken. Garden City: Doubleday, 1936. 43 – 54.

This story explores the unspoken power of mothers over their daughters' futures, a power which strengthens as daughters age if they are not able to individuate from their mothers. The spinster daughter in this narrative grieves when her mother comes close to death but then recuperates, for her death would have meant long-awaited freedom for 37-year-old Rebecca. When it seems as if her mother might die, Rebecca entertains thoughts of her own future she has suppressed for years under the burden of care for her mother. "It amazed Miss Rebecca when, in the midst of old Mrs. Simpson's illness, she had taken an absorbed delight in wondering what would happen to herself if her mother were to die," Haardt writes. "She felt sick and shaken at the great strangeness and yet life possessed a new marvel" (49). Rebecca begins to dream of what she will do with her freedom, but no definite plans come to mind. "The emotion was too new for that. It was enough to make lovely pictures of dangerous and wild things in her mind. It was the naked and raging feeling she was enjoying—not the thought process of planning" (50). When the doctor announces Mrs. Simpson will live, Rebecca is relieved, even glad, "but the gladness was as heartless as laughter on the shadow of a sick-room" (50). Dreams of freedom have already taken hold in Rebecca and will not let go. Fascinated by the mysterious nature of medicine, she resolves to become a nurse, even taking steps toward arranging care for her mother so that she can begin nursing school. But the thrill of breaking away and beginning a career of her own is quickly overshadowed by the reality of her own fears of the unknown, masked even to herself with her careful rationalization that it would be heartless to leave someone as elderly as her mother.

128. Hara, Marie. "You in There." Sister Stew: Fiction and Poetry by Women. Eds. Juliet S. Kono and Cathy Song. Honolulu: Bamboo Ridge Press, 1991. 8 – 14.

Narrated from the perspective of a daughter talking to her semi-conscious, dying mother, this story presents an impassioned but ineffectual plea on the part of an adult daughter willing her mother to continue to live. Although her mother's emphysema is so widespread that the doctor has compared her trying to breathe to a person drowning, the daughter refuses to give up hope that her mother may yet recover. "Fear circles me," she confesses to her shriveled, motionless mother. "You need me to bolster, you, to talk you up and out of here. You need to connect to my energy. But first you must come back from wherever you are floating" (8). While the narrator enumerates all the opportunities her mother will miss if she does not survive—including her daughter's wedding and her eventual grandchildren—the only communication her mother offers are nonverbal signs that indicate she is no longer willing to fight to survive and is ready to die.

129. Hudson, Barbara. "The Arabesque." New Stories From the South: The Year's Best, 1991. Ed. Shannon Ravenel. Chapel Hill: Algonquin Books of Chapel Hill, 1991. 22 – 34.

Two daughters attempt to come to terms with the death of their mentally disturbed mother in this story. When the daughters were only four and nine years of age, their mother would often wake them in the middle of the night to clean house with Stravinsky's "The Firebird" resounding throughout the house. Although her craziness made their childhood difficult and unpredictable and the daughters experienced a sense of freedom and relief at her death, the past did not die with the passing of their mother; neither did their sense of loss fade away easily. Memories of their mother came floating back in the image of "women who laughed too hard, who were too kind, who had long fingers and dark hair" (32). Arden listens to "The Firebird" in the middle of the night when she cannot sleep and panics when she fears she cannot recall a memory of her mother clearly enough. It is Kate who advises her younger sister to "take your mother and you turn her into something else" to preserve that memory without losing her (34). To illustrate her analogy, Kate bends her body smoothly into a beautiful arabesque, and Arden begins to understand the meaning of her words of advice.

130. Hurst, Fannie. "She Walks in Beauty." The World's One Hundred Best Short Stories. New York: Funk and Wagnalls Company, 1927. 7 – 51.

A daughter tries to prevent her widowed mother's second marriage in this story, knowing that her mother's addiction to narcotics as a cure for her neuralgia pain will destroy her new relationship. Assuming the advising role of a well-intentioned mother, Alma tries to convince her mother she is not ready for marriage until her addiction is cured. " ' Alma's fighting with you, dearest,' " she assures her mother, " 'every inch of the way until—you're cured! And then—maybe—some day—anything you want! But not now' " (25). But like many daughters, Carrie ignores the advice of her daughter and remarries anyway, hopeful that a new husband with money will be her cure. But Carrie eventually destroys herself with her unsuccessful battle against her addiction, leaving her newly-married husband and daughter both alone with only a memory of a wife and mother.

131. Jarrett, Cora. "'To Be Burned at My Death.'" I Asked No Other Thing. New York: Farrar and Rinehart, 1937. 77 – 85.

A spinster daughter's final retaliation against her mother occurs after her mother's death in this story. Believing herself to be "her father's child," superior to her mother with her inherited charm, public spiritedness, and energy, Eula Trescott belittles her reticent mother as a fragile and indifferent woman, "careless about social service and disarmament and the welfare of the world" (80). At Olivia's death it is with pleasure that Eula turns the key to the desk drawer her mother always forbade her to open. Inside the once forbidden hiding place Eula discovers a bundle of letters her mother has requested "to be burned at my death." The letters reveal a woman her daughter has never known, a woman with two lovers but only one husband. Eula will do as her mother has requested and burn the letters—those "wicked, secret things, treasured for shameful years by the mother whom she and her father had revered and loved"—but not before she places the letters in her father's hands in hopes of diminishing his adoration for his wife and uplifting her own standing in his eyes.

132. Krysl, Marilyn. "Looking For Mother." Honey You've Been Dealt a Winning Hand. Santa Barbara: Capra Press, 1980. 92 – 101.

A daughter whose mother died of childbirth complications as she was born fantasizes variations of her mother's life and death in this story, desperately seeking a maternal connection in her life. The narrator imagines herself reading her mother's diary, discovered after her death, and sorting through the lingerie left in her her abandoned Chicago apartment as she searches for clues to the character of the woman she pictures in her mind as "bereft and beautiful," widowed by World War Two. Each image the narrator creates of her mother's life is later replaced by another, slightly revised version as she continually seeks to piece together a composite of the mother she never knew.

133. Le Guin, Ursula K. "Crosswords." Searoad: Chronicles of Klatsand. New York: Harper Collins, 1991. 111 – 118.

The adult daughter in this story, haunted by memories of her estranged mother who died without her knowledge, seeks to reestablish ties with her own daughter before the tragedy has a chance to repeat itself. After she learns of her mother's death, the narrator tries to piece together the few memories she has remaining that will help her to know her mother. "It was as if I had something to puzzle out, kind of like a crossword," the narrator explains, "where you have a word down, say, but you haven't figured out the ones across it. I like crosswords. Often I'd do the one in the paper, those long nights. I did them to keep from thinking, because whatever I started thinking about, it would end up with my mother" (116). She carries the vision of her mother with her at all times following her death, even assuming her bodily image at times, as she tries to "listen to what I didn't hear" when her mother was still alive (118).

134. Linett, Deena. "Gifts." Ms. March 1978. 67 – 71.

The daughter who narrates this story relates her feelings and reactions as she witnesses her mother's death and helps prepare her body for burial. As the "last act of loving kindness" she can give her mother, the narrator joins her father in performing the difficult task of washing her mother's body and clothing it in a shroud. As the narrator enters the room where her mother's body lies, she fears she will disappoint her father and not be able to find the emotional strength to accompany him, as she has promised. "I had never seen anyone who was dead before," she writes of the experience. "I was stunned and terrified that I would scream, or cry; fail him and her" (71). At first she cannot bring herself to touch her mother's body but gradually she overcomes her reluctance and assists her father as together they carefully complete the "last act of loving kindness" they can offer her mother.

135. Lyles, Lois F. "Last Christmas Gift From a Mother." Double Stitch: Black Women Write About Mothers & Daughters. Eds. Patricia Bell-Scott, Berly Guy-Sheftall, Jacqueline Jones Royster, Janet Sims-Wood, Miriam DeCosta-Willis, and Lucie Fultz. Boston: Beacon Press, 1991. 241 – 251.

This narrative traces the gradual demise of a 63-year-old black mother to cancer, as witnessed by her grieving daughter whose relationship with her mother changes dramatically during this time. Although the narrator will not cry in the presence of her father and son, for she would surely be reproached by them for demonstrating her "weakness of sorrow," when she is alone with her mother, they share their mutual emotions and openly cry together. "She doesn't mind my tears, I know, " the narrator writes, "and hers don't bother me. When nobody is looking at us, we can cry, and then it is all right" (242). Although the daughter-narrator's parents sheltered her from pain and suffering as a child, her mother now looks upon this shared experience of her dying as a maternal gift she can offer her adult daughter—an opportunity for her to test her own emotional strength. "She is letting me see if I am strong enough to grapple, by proxy, with Death," writes the narrator (247).

But such a gift is difficult to accept with grace. After her mother's stroke, the narrator berates herself for not being able to look at her mother's deformed face directly. "Since the stroke," she writes, "I have not kissed her hands or face. Did I promise that I'd always be her support, no matter what happened? Well, I lied. I am afraid of her now. *Liar, liar,* I taunt myself, You only loved a woman beautiful or whole" (249 – 250). In many respects, the daughter has reversed roles with her mother, who has now become as physically helpless as an infant. The daughter cleans up her mother's urine while she washes parts of her mother's body she has never seen. "Her sex is a forlorn, desiccated rose in a desert of loose, sandy flesh," the daughter describes her mother. "Her privates simultaneously repel, shame, and fascinate me. I cannot remember ever having seen my mother's nakedness. *This is the body from which I came* " (251). Although her mother's body fails, the narrator takes solace in the fact that her mother retains her mental alertness, even as she is dying.

136. Marello, Laura. "Catch Me Go Looking." New Directions in Prose and Poetry 53. Ed. J. Laughlin. New York: New Directions, 1989. 88 – 121.

In this innovative story—blending past and present, thought and memory—an adolescent daughter seeks to know and understand her mother, who committed suicide when her daughter was still a child. With only sketchy details offered by her father, who is reluctant to answer her many questions, the daughter delves into her own past memories, mixing fact with fiction, dreams with reality, to try to make tangible the mother whose image becomes more blurred as time passes.

137. McClain, Judith. "Prayer." Iowa Woman. Autumn 1990: 19 – 23.

A mother who witnesses the "perverse" tragedy of her daughter dying before she does vows to build a close relationship with her granddaughter that she never experienced with her own daughter. Looking at Grace in mourning for her mother, the mother-narrator searches her granddaughter's face to see how much of her daughter she might still find there. For a moment it seems as if Grace has become her daughter, and there is the chance to start over and rectify past wrongs. But it is her granddaughter with whom the narrator must look to establish the relationship she never had with her daughter.

138. Moore, Lorrie. "What Is Seized." Self-Help. New York: Alfred A. Knopf, 1985. 23 – 46.

At her mother's death, the daughter-narrator of this narrative offers a collage of memories from old photographs and childhood memories that create the impression of a sensitive woman, unhappy for much of her life because she married a "cold man" who was incapable of demonstrating emotion, a woman who eventually ended up divorced and alone. " 'Beware of a man,' " the narrator's mother warns her, " 'who says he loves you but who is incapable of a passionate confession, of melting into a sob' " (43). Such insights are the riches that daughters inherit from mothers, the narrator writes:

> Once they die, of course, you get the strand of pearls, the blue quilt, some of the original wedding gifts—a tray shellacked with the invitation, an old rusted toaster—but the touches and the words and the moaning the night she dies, these are what you seize, save, carry around in little invisible envelopes, opening them up quickly, like a carnival huckster, giving the world a peek. They will not stay quiet. No matter how you try, no matter how you lick them. The envelopes will not stay glued. (39 – 40)

139. Morgan, Kay. "The Crowd Upstairs." Calyx. 12.2 (1989/90): 62 – 71.

This narrative describes the reactions of an adolescent daughter to her mother's terminal illness and gradual loss of sanity and her father's insistence that life is a dream. "Crazy as my mother was, or seemed," writes the narrator, "her world was still easier to share than way my father's. I simply pretended to agree with her firm belief that a crowd of starving people lived upstairs—people who were at their loudest and most ravenous in the early hours of the morning" (62). Her mother's delusions of the "crowd upstairs" seem so real at times the narrator has to remind herself that their presence is only in her mother's mind. With loving patience and acceptance of the "crowd upstairs," the father and daughter in this story care for her dying mother as both her body and mind succumb to disease.

140. Nunes, Susan. "A Small Obligation." Passages to the Dream Shore: Short Stories of Contemporary Hawaii. Ed. Frank Stewart. Honolulu: University of Hawaii Press, 1987. 147 – 156.

This narrative examines the frustrations of a Japanese-American mother caring for her own aging mother and how those feelings affect her relationship with her daughter. At the age of 92, her mother's mind and body are failing, her memories jumbled and distorted with lengthy time lapses, her need for attention almost constant; yet she refuses to consider nursing home placement. The mother vows to her own daughter that she will never saddle her with such a burden, that she and her husband will use their meager savings to provide for themselves in old age; thus, her daughter can expect no inheritance from her parents. The daughter feels as if she has been struck by her mother's displaced anger. "Is it my imagination," the daughter wonders, "or is she attacking me? I cannot escape the feeling that I, that we, are being punished for something. But what is it, what is it we are supposed to have done? We are a family of unspoken obligations. I don't know what, but I am stung" (154). In this family, where so many words remain unsaid and so much must be inferred, the daughter is left uncertain about her relationship with her mother, even as she is losing her grandmother.

141. Oates, Joyce Carol. "Back There." Where Are You Going, Where Have You Been? Stories of Young America. Greenwich: Fawcett Publications, 1974. 293 – 314.

The adult daughter who narrates this story returns to the home of her youth to confront the possibility of her mother's death, even as she relives painful adolescent memories of the night she was raped "back there." During her visit with her mother she writes: "My mother and I became friends again, tentative and polite as young girls, unsure of each other" (297). But the need to keep the conversation flowing becomes a strain, she confesses: "I felt slightly hypnotized. I felt a certain danger, that I would say to her quite calmly, 'Please don't die. Don't die. Don't do that to my father and me. Not yet'" (298). Before her mother dies, the narrator feels the need to explain to this woman the circumstances and choices of her life, a mixture of truth and lies carefully blended to increase her chances of maternal approval. When her mother expresses concern for her husband and daughter's future happiness, the narrator experiences a sudden "flash of rage: to want us to be happy, to expect that we could be happy! What a tyranny it was, this apologetic, inexorable, hopeless hope of mothers!" (299).

142. Ozick, Cynthia. "The Shawl." The Shawl. New York: Alfred A. Knopf, 1989. 3 – 10.

The incarcerated mother in this story witnesses the brutal slaying of her young daughter by a Nazi concentration camp guard during World War Two. Aware that her daughter would be killed if discovered in the camp, Rosa Lublin conceals baby Magda in the folds of her shawl for several months without discovery. When Magda's presence is discovered, however, Rosa stands horrified and powerless while a guard repeatedly heaves her daughter's tiny, emaciated body against a wall. Rejecting the maternal voice within urging her to try to save the life of her daughter, Rosa stuffs the fibers of the shawl into her own mouth to stifle her screams of agony, knowing that if she tried to intervene on behalf of her daughter, her efforts would be futile and she would only forfeit her own life as well.

143. Paley, Grace. "Mother." My Mother's Daughter: Stories by Women. Ed. Irene Zahava. Freedom, CA: The Crossing Press, 1991. 229 – 230.

The daughter who narrates this story identifies with the lyrics of the song, "Oh, I Long to See My Mother in the Doorway" when she hears the melody playing on the radio. After losing her mother during late adolescence, she writes: "Naturally for the rest of my life I longed to see her, not only in doorways, in a great number of places—in the dining room with my aunts, at the window looking up and down the block, in the country garden among zinnias and marigolds, in the living room with my father" (230). It is only in these imaginary scenes that she can now fantasize the image of her mother.

144. Phillips, Jayne Anne. "Souvenir." Black Tickets. New York: Delacorte Press, 1979. 177 – 196.

"Souvenir" is the story of a mother and adult daughter coming to gracefully accept the eventuality of the mother's death. Although

Kate honors her brother's wishes and promises him she will not reveal the severity of her mother's condition to her, she feels she is betraying her mother by avoiding the truth. "The secrets were a travesty," she thinks. "What if there were things her mother wanted done, people she needed to see? Kate wanted to wake her before these hours passed in the dark and confess that she had lied. Between them, through the tension, there had always been a trusted clarity. Now it was twisted" (190 – 191). But her children's attempt to conceal the truth is unnecessary, Kate's mother reveals. Sensing the unspoken gravity of her condition, she reveals her intuition to her daughter. " 'I know all about it,' " she confesses. " 'I know what you haven't told me' " (196). Phillips' story portrays with sensitivity the difficulty of both mother and daughter admitting and accepting the eventual end of their relationship.

145. Reely, Mary Katharine. "Hands." Golden Tales of the Prairie States. Ed. May Lamberton Becker. New York: Dodd, Mead and Company, 1932. 121 – 136.

A niece cares for her critically ill aunt and prepares her body for death as she would have liked to have done for her own deceased mother in this story. When Calla made the decision to move her mother from the rural Midwest to the city to care for her as she aged, her mother was so unhappy with life there that she escaped, only to die alone before she could reach her hometown. Criticized by the townspeople as an unfaithful daughter, Calla returns after nine years as her aunt is on the verge of death to perform the necessary duties that a daughter would assume for her dying mother. Those who witness her calm and competent acceptance of this responsibility see Calla's deceased mother still living in the form of her daughter. It is her hands, Calla confesses, that automatically knew what to do when they closed her aunt's eyes, straightened her withered limbs, washed her shrunken body, and dressed her without the need of direction. "My brain didn't work. But my hands did. They knew what to do. They knew" (133 – 134). The maternal instincts which often direct women's behavior unconsciously guide and sustain the niece in this story through an emotionally difficult period in which she must prove herself a competent and caring daughter to those who have cast doubts on her devotion.

146. Roberts, Nancy. "A Proper Introduction." Women and Other Bodies of Water. Port Townsend, WA: Dragon Gate, Inc., 1987. 47 – 60.

The adult daughter who narrates this story regrets that she never had a "proper introduction" to her mother before she died of multiple sclerosis. She avoided her mother during the last few months before her death, the narrator realizes, because she would have felt vulnerable to be closer. She writes in retrospect:

> It was as if my visits to my mother tore off a layer that kept me from feeling the world's dangers—or from a great rage and sorrow endangering from within. Uncovered, too, was the worry that I didn't really love her, not enough anyhow to stop avoiding her. Yet Mother had approved in her way. When I was "myself," I was competent, everyone said, talented, and even independent. "You're the strong one in the family," she used to tell me. To remain so, I had avoided her. (48)

Since her death, the daughter searches among her mother's possessions for traces of the mother who always encouraged her to be independent ("Find out what you really want. . . . Know what you can do, how you can be strong," her mother would advise), yet had so little independence herself (53). After her family rejects her idea of a sitting shiva for her mother as unchristian and she can find no one at her mother's memorial service who might want to talk about her (the minister only mentions her mother's name once between the Lord's Prayer and the Twenty-Third Psalm, just before the benediction), the daughter scatters the ashes in a nearby stream of a woman who disappeared from her life before they were ever properly introduced as mother and daughter.

147. Ryerson, Alice. "Do Not Disturb." Best Stories from New Writers. Ed. Linda S. Sanders. Cincinnati: Writer's Digest Books, 1989. 178 – 187.

The daughter in this semi-autobiographical story honors her mother's wish to choose when and how she will die by allowing her the freedom to commit suicide without interruption. In preparation for the time when she will need them, the aging mother, once an artist, carries a woven bag which contains two bottles of pills, prayers, and a list of ways to kill oneself. She entrusts her daughter with this valuable bag, afraid that "nurses or doctors will dispose of it—all those carefully stored up sleeping pills," the daughter-narrator writes. "She is even afraid that her husband, my stepfather, might take it away. She is afraid that they will all keep her alive too long. Longer than she can draw" (180). When the daughter senses that the night of her mother's suicide has arrived—when pain pills are no longer effective, when goodbyes to all family members have been said, when no more pictures can be drawn, the daughter makes a difficult decision. She chooses to do nothing, for she realizes she cannot have a part in this one-act drama dictated by her mother, that to try to persuade her to change her mind would violate her mother's wishes. Yet the narrator cannot bear to stay with her mother, knowing what she is about to do, although she knows her mother would appreciate her daughter's presence. "I leave her," she writes, "the way one leaves a beloved child alone to choose her own dress for the party" to allow to perform the act she has chosen in privacy (186).

In the "Notes" accompanying this story, the editors comment on the difficult role assigned to the daughter-narrator of the story. She must accept that "she cannot stop what is to happen and cannot take part in it. She can't pull off the dramatic death scene in a darkened bedroom her mother would like. She can't keep her from having to go to the hospital one last time. She can't even find the right words to say. But she *can* do nothing" (188). The editors note that in the writing of this story, which won an Illinois Literary Arts Council Award, Ryerson "has accomplished one of the most difficult tasks of fiction: she has taken an extremely personal event from her own life and written about it in a way that transcends the particulars of what happened. She has written a story that is about more than her mother's death, or even this character's death, but rather about something universal—loss, grief, and our inability to protect ourselves from them" (188).

148. Shinner, Peggy. "If I Lived in Maine." My Mother's Daughter: Stories by Women. Ed. Irene Zahava. Freedom, CA: The Crossing Press, 1991. 189 – 195.

A lesbian daughter feels a sense of guilt and responsibility for the approaching death of her mother in this story because stress is known to cause cancer, and "I remember that she said I cause her stress because I'm a lesbian," the daughter-narrator writes. "Stress causes cancer. That's what she said. At the very least suggested. She implied it. Even if she couldn't say it. She hinted" (189). The narrator remembers her mother berating her as a child for her lack of affection and warmth. "She said I was like no daughter no mother ever had," the narrator recalls. Yet a recurring vision that is perhaps a memory, or perhaps just a wish or desire, plays over and over in the narrator's mind in which their mother-daughter bond is reassured with an exchange of displayed emotion. Her mother is lying in a hospital bed shortly before her death and gives her daughter a smile. "I thought it was a smile," the daughter writes. "A slight, sad upturning. She didn't ask me to kiss her but I would have. I would have forced myself" (195).

149. Sikes, Shirley. "Sentimental Journal." Calyx. 13.1 (1990/91). 83 – 92.

This narrative records the reactions of a daughter as she witnesses her mother gradually deteriorating with Alzheimer's disease. Interspersed with hospital and nursing home scenes of patients such as the narrator's mother who have forgotten how to swallow and chew, who suffer from paranoid delusions, who cannot remember yesterday's events, are the narrator's memories of happier times when her mother was young and vibrant, a woman proud to have been born of "pioneer stock." As her mother begins to eat less and less, hardly speaking during her daughter's visits, the narrator pauses to reflect on the relationship of the mind and death:

> I wonder what goes on in the brain when arteries get hard and inflexible. Can it be that moments of stimulation create new circuits and ideas get through?
>
> What an immense space minds are!
>
> Can it be there is a kind of sun there and it gradually dies? Can it be there is an inner migration—but again, away from us? (91)

150. Simon, Rachel. "The Greatest Mystery of Them All." Little Nightmares, Little Dreams. Boston: Houghton Mifflin, 1990. 37 – 51.

The 14-year-old daughter who narrates this story, shot by her drug-dealing mother for attempting to thwart her business, observes the world below from her the windows of her new home in heaven. While she ponders the big questions of life, such as evolution and religion, she spend most of her time trying to decipher the actions of her own mother—"the greatest mystery of them all" (44). When drug dealing leads to her mother's death as well, the narrator anticipates her arrival in heaven with ambivalence. "It's after midnight," she writes, "but that's all right. I'll wait up for her till dawn if I have to. I don't mind. I want to be here when she gets in, so I can hug her hello, and tell her I'm OK. And let her see how much she worried me. And finally give her a piece of my mind" (51).

151. Spencer, Elizabeth. "First Dark." Ship Island and Other Stories. New York: McGraw-Hill, 1968. 1 – 27.

An aging, invalid mother commits suicide so that her daughter is free to marry in this short story. Although Mrs. Harvey approves of her daughter's choice of mate and grants her daughter the freedom to marry, Frances cannot reconcile the responsibilities she would continue to have caring for her irascible mother with the prospect of becoming a wife. " 'I can't leave her, Tom,' " she confesses to her future husband. " 'Of all the horrible ideas! She'd make demands, take all my time, laugh at you behind your back—she has to run everything. You'd hate me in a week' " (17). But Mrs. Harvey's sudden death, which her daughter discovers later to be a carefully planned suicide, sets free her daughter to begin a new life of independence from her mother.

152. Tetu, Randeane. "Graves of the Daughters." Merle's & Marilyn's Mink Ranch. Watsonville, CA: Papier-Machine Press, 1991. 64 – 66.

A childless mother and her husband fantasize about the daughters they never gave birth to in this story. Driving to a nearby cemetery to visit their daughters' graves, Aurelia and Howard discuss the daughters they were never able to conceive but imagine buried here. " 'Ella had such a lovely voice,' " comments Aurelia. " 'Always singing. Always cheerful.' " " 'And Carlotta,' " her husband adds. " 'Remember when she thought she could fly and skinned her knees flying out of the apple tree?' " (64). Howard imagines his daughters inherited their beauty from their mother as husband and wife perpetuate the fantasy that they were once mother and father and outlived their daughters.

153. Townsend, Ruth. "The Jimsons." Iowa Woman. Nov/Dec 1980: 24 – 26.

A farm wife mourning the loss of her mother shortly after her burial wages her own war against mortality in this story as she attacks the killer jimson weeds invading her Iowa bean field. Mil remembers when she first held the beautiful yet ugly blossom of the jimson flower. The white blossoms with delicate lavender veins reminded her of stars which would have made her mother want to sing. But Mil's husband had kicked the jimson blossom into the dirt declaring that he'd like to "kill them all," for the jimson weed was "the worst weed there is" (25). Now Mil finds herself hating jimsons too, for their deadly power over that which is still living. "They grew and grew until they killed whatever was in the field. They killed people too. They would kill her someday. They were the farm and the work and the beauty that wasn't beauty when you got close and found out all about it" (25). In a cathartic purge of rage at the death of her mother and her husband's insensitivity to her grief as well as the broader concern of inevitability of death for all living things, Mil leaves behind her unwashed dishes and begins pulling the jimson weeds, hating their destructive power but admiring their individual beauty until her husband's demanding voice recalls her to present duties.

154. Vaughn, Stephanie. "My Mother Breathing Light." Sweet Talk. New York: Random House, 1990. 58 – 78.

An adult daughter witnesses her mother's preparation for death in this story. At first the aging mother refuses to say the word "cancer," masking the truth behind safer words such as "blockage" and "development." But as she gradually begins to accept the inevitability of her approaching death, the mother's actions signify to her daughter that she is preparing for the end of her life, even as she fights the specter of death. No words need to be spoken. The mother carefully removes all the pictures of herself from the family photo album which she feels are unflattering, "expurgating the ugly likenesses of herself in order to leave an attractive vision for me when she is gone" (72). She dreams of flying to expensive Swiss mineral baths and Mexican health spas while she secretly reads self-help survival guides and drinks healthful concoctions of "everything she has ever heard was good for one's health" each morning in her search for the elusive miracle cure that will sustain her life. As both mother and daughter become aware of the "secret that each of us keep from the other," it is the daughter who assumes the traditional role of the mother—"strong, cheerful, controlling a small bubble of space in which there is no time, only light and warmth" (78). While trying to provide emotional support for her mother, the daughter clings to the hopeful belief that "we never die alone" as her only comfort in the loss of her mother.

155. Villegas, Anna Tuttle. "Do Not Go Gentle." Iowa Woman. Summer 1984: 19 – 23.

The aging and immobile mother who narrates this story describes the limited space that has become her world as she senses her own death is approaching. Her daughter-teacher is one of four people who "live my life for me" as they enter and exit the room that has become her home. "Her slender hands," she writes of her daughter, "remind me of my own—not these which sit gnarled on the flowered pillow in my lap—my real hands, my doing hands" (20). On a nearby desk within her view, the mother can still see a picture of her daughter at the age of 20 and herself "double her age, though young." She recalls memories of the seconds that occurred immediately after the flash of the shutter. "I have these carefully stored remembrances tucked away so that a pine tree or a gold picture frame can give them back. I don't need eyes to see these scenes. Even my window's peripheries don't box in these my real truths" (21). As the aging woman faces the inevitability of her death, she envisions how the four people left in her life will each react to her passing. It is her daughter's imagined reaction that interests her most, for she looks upon the experience as an opportunity for growth and maturity which she selfishly wishes she could witness in person:

> My daughter will weep as good daughters should. Her grief will not pass like the others' but will transform itself into a different kind of measure. . . . She'll gain from my death, I'm sure, and I grow angry to think that I am cheated of seeking that final growth, the setting-in of the poise and grace of maturity. (23)

156. Warner, Sharon Oard. "A Simple Matter of Hunger." Iowa Woman. Spring 1991: 23 – 28.

A foster mother begins a relationship with her new AIDS-infected daughter in this story as she realizes she must also accept the inevitable, premature death of this infant. Just as Jancey's real mother lies dying in a hospital of AIDS, so does her abandoned daughter exhibit symptoms that the disease has invaded her tiny body. For all the love and affection the narrator-mother can offer her foster-daughter, she must face the reality that Jancey will always remain "just out of my reach" like the birds she remembers soaring through the fields of her youth.

157. Yolen, Jane. "Names." Tales of Wonder. New York: Schocken Books, 1983. 253 – 258.

The daughter of a Holocaust survivor in this story carries on the traditional mourning of Jewish victims ritualized by her mother and sacrifices herself at age 13 in what she perceives as an act of daughterly devotion. Even before Rachel was brought into the world, she heard her mother continually chant the recitation of names of Holocaust victims and grew up learning the stories behind each of the names. But the continuation of this tradition is not enough to please Rachel's mother. Rachel must do more to make her mother smile. When she reaches adolescence, Rachel gradually realizes what she must do. She gradually starves herself, becoming another casualty of the Holocaust who never lived in Nazi Germany but is nevertheless victimized by her mother's obsession with the Holocaust tragedy.

Sources:

Kandik, Karen. "Finding Home." Loss of the Ground-Note: Women Writing About the Loss of Their Mothers. Ed. Helen Vozenilek. Los Angeles: Clothespin Fever Press, 1992. 166 – 169.

Townsend, Alison. "Small Comforts: An Essay on Mary." Loss of the Ground-Note: Women Writing About the Loss of Their Mothers. Ed. Helen Vozenilek. Los Angeles: Clothespin Fever Press, 1992. 107 – 122.

Vozenilek, Helen, ed. Introduction. Loss of the Ground-Note: Women Writing About the Loss of Their Mothers. Los Angeles: Clothespin Fever Press, 1992. 7 – 10.

5

Expectations

INTRODUCTION

By virtue of their closeness and similarity of roles as women, mothers and daughters develop certain expectations of one another, a tradition that can lead to frustration and disappointment if those expectations are unrealistic. In the majority of the stories included in this chapter, the mother-daughter relationship becomes strained because expectations of either mother or daughter are not met. Only in stories written by Elizabeth Evans and Lucy Huffaker where mothers sacrifice their expectations and accept their daughters' individual choices are potential conflicts between mothers and daughters resolved amicably.

In several of the stories included in this chapter, mothers attempt to force their daughters into prescribed roles. The Chinese-American mother in Amy Tan's "Two Kinds" tries to mold her daughter into a child prodigy, giving her young daughter the misconception that as she grows up she will eventually become perfect. The daughter-narrator's obvious imperfections bring extreme disappointment to the mother whose expectations of perfection in her daughter are shattered, but joy to the daughter who revels in the discovery of her own individuality, regardless of how flawed it might be, as a personal possession that is beyond the control of her mother. The mother in Gayle Whittier's "Turning Out" is so disappointed that her daughter fails to develop into the talented ballernia she envisioned her daughter would become that she contemplates giving birth to another child as a second attempt at creating the daughter of her expectations. The mother in S. L. Wisenberg's "Pageant" pressures her eight-year-old daughter to enter a series of oratory contests, striking her out of frustration when Ceci's performance fails to match her expectations. Without the assurance of maternal approval and support, Ceci begins to convince herself that no one will ever understand her, least of all her mother. The black mother in Shirley Ann Grau's "The Other Way" forces her child to remain in an all-white school, despite her social ostracism there, so that she can grow up to compete in a predominantly white society. Thus Sandra Lee faces a long and lonely adolescence in order to meet the expectations of her mother. In Emily Prager's "A Visit From the Footbinder" a Chinese empress continues the ancient tradition of footbinding, ordering the painful procedure to be performed on her youngest daughter at the age of six to ensure that her foot size will be the expected length for an acceptable bride in society.

Mothers in stories authored by Karen Brown, Jean McCord, and Tillie Olsen anticipate better opportunities for their daughters than fate has dealt them. The mother in Brown's "Destiny" hopes her daughter will be spared the hopeless cycle of unfulfilling jobs and undesirable males that have characterized her life so far. The mother in McCord's "I Left I All Behind When I Ran" envisions her daughter becoming the artist she once dreamed she would be. And the mother portrayed in Tillie Olsen's "I Stand Here Ironing" hopes that the life of her oldest daughter will not become an extension of her own life of poverty and disappointment.

In contrast to these hopeful maternal characters, the mother in Jamaica Kincaid's "Girl" holds no positive expectations for her daughter to escape poverty and develop a more promising future for herself. This mother passes on a legacy of self-survival tactics she knows her daughter will need in order to survive in the harsh environment where she will probably live for the rest of her life.

Mothers in stories written by Djuana Barnes, Gloria Naylor, and Shirley A. Williams experience intense disappointment when their daughters fail to meet their expectations. The estranged but worldly mother in Barnes's "Aller et Retour" fears her adolescent daughter will never experience the extremes of life, her world has been so sheltered by her father's protective childrearing. The black mother in Naylor's "Kiswana Browne" disapproves of her daughter's involvement in the black movement which she predicts will never evolve into a revolution and bring about the social changes that Kiswana envisions for her race. Another black mother in Williams's "Tell Martha Not to Moan" is disappointed when her daughter does not live up to the expectations associated with her biblical name. " 'Martha,' " she explains to her daughter, unwed and pregnant for the second time, " 'I named you after that woman in the Bible cause I want you to be like her. Be good in the same way she is' " (133).

Although the daughters in stories written by Elizabeth Evans, Lucy Huffaker, and Claudia Smith Brinson do not fit the prescribed molds their daughters originally envisioned for them, the mothers in these stories allow their daughters the freedom of independence to become whoever they want to be. The overprotective mother in "The Sleeping Gypsy" may disapprove of her college-aged daughter's choice of a nontraditional lifestyle, but she comes to respect her daughter's need for freedom to establish her own identity at this stage in her life. The mother of eight children in Huffaker's "The Way of Life" faces the possible loss of her dream for her daughter to become a great pianist when she honors her desire for marriage instead. The traditional mother in Brinson's award-winning "Einstein's Daughter" releases her unconventional daughter to discover her own sense of self and space somewhere out in the universe.

The expectations of motherhood itself are a disappointment to the young mother in Sheila Kohler's "A Quiet Place" whose romantic perceptions of playing mother are shattered by the demands and self-sacrifices involved in raising two daughters.

Daughters can also experience disappointment when their mothers fail to meet their expectations, stories authored by Alice Booth, Lenore Marshall, and Lynne Sharon Schwartz demonstrate. The college-aged daughters in Booth's "Mother and the Girls" never expect their mother to become their rival when they invite her to become their housekeeper at college. Yet the mother in this story begins to recognize her own need for self-actualization and discovers ways to fulfill herself in this academic atmosphere, even though her daughters resent her intrusion into what they perceive as endeavors for younger women only. The young daughter in Marshall's "The Closed Door" learns that her mother is less than perfect and very capable of shutting her daughter out of her private life, if only temporarily, in order to fulfill her own desires. The introverted, adolescent daughter in Schwartz's "Over the Hill" is resentful of her mother's active social life and jealous of the time she spends socializing with her male and female companions; a 34-year-old woman is "over the hill" in her estimation, much too old to be leading such a lifestyle.

SHORT FICTION

158. Barnes, Djuana. "Aller et Retour." Selected Works of Djuna Barnes. New York: Farrar, Straus and Cudahy, 1962. 3 – 11.

A mother's extreme disappointment in the development of her estranged daughter is evident in this story. Madame von Bartmann returns to Nice from Russia when her estranged husband dies to reunite with her daughter for the first time in seven years. " 'I'll have to see what he has made of you,' " she remarks to Richter as she examines her adolescent daughter (7). What Madame von Bartmann discovers is a child who has become a woman during her absence but in a very sheltered, protective environment with little contact with the outside world. Richter, to the horror of her mother, has never experienced the extremes of life. " 'Life,' " Madame von Bartmann explains to her daughter, " 'is filthy; it is also frightful. There is everything in it: murder, pain, beauty, disease—death. Do you know this?' " (9). Imploring her daughter to experience every aspect of life possible, she advises her daughter, most of all to " 'Think everything, good, bad, indifferent; everything, and do everything, everything! Try to know what you are before you die. And come back to me a good woman' " (10). When Richter quietly announces her engagement to a governmental clerk who has assured her a secure but eventless life as a homemaker, Madame von Bartmann realizes the course of her daughter's life has already been cast during her absence, and she can no longer influence its direction. She is forced to accept the disappointing realization that although her daughter may live, she will probably never fully experience life as her mother envisions it should be.

159. Becker, Robin. "In the Badlands." The Things that Divide Us. Eds. Faith Conlon, Rachel da Silva, and Barbara Wilson. Seattle: Seal Press, 1985. 15 – 26.

The mother who narrates this story reluctantly but gradually comes to accept her daughter's lesbian relationship and her choice of mate. When Carol first brings home her female lover, her mother wonders if Helen is worthy of her daughter and doubts that a young, urban woman can adapt to the harshness of South Dakota life, especially during the winter months. At times her disapproval of Helen causes conflicts between her daughter and herself; at other times they become competitors for Carol's affections. The narrator begins to realize that her rejection of Helen has more to do with her own inability to let her daughter transcend into adulthood and her own fear of being closed out of her daughter's life than it does with her choice of mate, who proves to be an adaptable and caring woman.

160. Booth, Alice. "Mother and the Girls." Mother in Modern Story. Ed. Maud Van Buren and Katharine Isabel Bemis. New York: Century Company, 1928. 3 – 21,

A mother becomes an unexpected rival of her college-aged daughters in this short story. When Helen and Isabel decide to rent their own apartment while attending college but discover that cooking and housekeeping are unwelcome intrusions into their busy routines, they invite their mother to come live with them to serve as their housekeeper—an "object of charity" of sorts. But their mother-housekeeper surprises them when she decides to trade her dressmaking career to earn the college degree she never completed 20 years earlier when she was suddenly widowed with two small daughters. Despite Helen and Isabel's disapproval and fear that their mother will be an embarrassment, she proves herself capable of college academics as well as housekeeping. In her writing Brown explores the conflicts that result when mothers and daughters a generation apart in age are placed on the same competitive plane. Simultaneously, Brown develops the characterization of a woman who makes significant sacrifices in her life to raise her daughters single-handedly but also recognizes her own needs for self-fulfillment and pursues them, despite the objections of her daughters, who are too absorbed in their own lives to recognize their mother is an individual with needs as well, someone more than an "object of charity."

161. Brinson, Claudia Smith. "Einstein's Daughter." Prize Stories 1990: The O. Henry Awards. Ed. William Abrahams. New York: Doubleday, 1990. 301 – 314.

The daughter-narrator of this story moves back and forth in a time travel of the imagination to discover her sense of self and space. Leaving her parents "to their own time zones," she creates her own, "filled with desire and impatience, determined to lose myself in the space of sky and sea" (313). She knows she is not the daughter her mother would have desired or even expected. "To her I am a mystery," the narrator confesses, "a mutation, a miracle unawked for; to me she is mass unconverted, gravity's penalty, my immutable mother" (312). Her mother of traditional values would have been happier with a more conventional daughter with less restless desires. " 'Don't go looking for trouble, young lady, and it won't find you,' " she warns her roving daughter. " 'Your duty is to love people and to serve people, and you don't do that if you're galivanting around. You give and you do what you can, and you make sure it's good. That's enough for a woman. Love is enough' " (307). But love is not enough for this daughter of flight. " 'I'm not going to let gravity wreck me,' " she defies her mother. " 'The more you try to tie me to you, the faster I'm going to go' " (311). Unable to compromise, the mother in this story releases her enigmatic daughter to create the only possible destination suitable for a daughter of Einstein—"a now of my own making. She has let go of me as we both knew she would," the narrator writes. "What will she do without me? I dare not stop to ask" (314).

162. Brown, Alice. "A Flower of April." Country Neighbors. Boston: Houghton Mifflin, 1910. 42 – 52.

Her maternal ties are used as an excuse to avoid relationships with young males by the shy daughter portrayed in this story. While other young women her age begin the courtship process and look forward to marriage, Ellen clings to the love of her mother while she shuns the advances of potential suitors. " 'Mother,' " Ellen entreats her mother, " 'I needn't ever be with anybody but you, need I?' " " 'No, no,' " Ellen's mother assures her, " 'you're mother's own girl' "(48). The mother-daughter bond in this story serves to prevent Ellen from following the customary course of courtship and marriage. As she remains sheltered by her lonely, protective mother, Ellen tries to convince herself that maternal love is the only kind of love she needs to fulfill her life.

163. Brown, Karen. "Destiny." The New Family: The Graywolf Annual Eight. Ed. Scott Walker. St. Paul: Graywolf Press, 1991. 63 – 73.

The mother who narrates this story, having experienced several failed relationships, including one with the father of her daughter who presently "doesn't even know we're alive," expresses the hope that her daughter will not fall into the same hopeless cycle of unfulfilling jobs and unpredictable men that has comprised her adult life. She writes:

> I've vowed that I will not let Marianne be fooled like I was. I've been trying to set an example—staying chaste, uninvolved—but sometimes I find myself imagining Marianne years from now, at fifteen: brown hair streaming under violet streetlights, a silver charm bracelet jingling on her write, staring up at someone's face, or at the moon . . . and I ache with jealousy, with a mysterious excitement that has nothing to do with my life in the past. I'm fooling myself, of course. I already know that Marianne is the only thing I can love and not pay for, ultimately, with my soul. (63).

As Marianne matures, her mother recognizes, "she too will be learning the cycle of things, the irresistible wheel that drew us into its spokes" (73). Perhaps hers will be a more fortunate cycle than her mother's.

164. Evans, Elizabeth. "The Sleeping Gypsy." Locomotion. St. Paul: New Rivers Press, 1986. 9 – 19.

An overprotective mother begins to accept her daughter's individuality and need for independence in this story. Disappointed that her daughter, once a thoughtful child and promising scholar, quits college to work in a junk store when she envisioned her building a successful career, marriage and social life, the mother gradually learns to accept the fact that her daughter will never fit the mold she has prescribed for her. Although the mother cringes at her daughter's offbeat taste in men and nontraditional lifestyle, she realizes that what her daughter needs most at this stage in her life is the freedom to establish her own identity and respect for her individuality.

165. Fisher, M. K. F. "Another Love Story." Sister Age. New York: Vintage Books, 1983. 59 – 82.

The young daughters in this story attempt to convince their divorced mother to remarry because they need a father replacement. " 'The thing is,' " one of the daughters proposes earnestly, " 'that it would be good for all three of us to know a man to be with. Holly and I are still too young to be married. But you're not too old, I guess' " (75). After discarding the fat milkman as a possible replacement, the daughters continue their search until they discover the perfect mate while vacationing at the seashore. The daughters unanimously recommend that their mother marry a local beach wanderer they have befriended who promises to be a compassionate and playful father replacement. Although his proposal to Mrs. Allen to be a friend and helpmate in marriage is tempting, she begins to realize as she observes her daughters interacting with Mr. Henshaw that it is her daughters he loves, not herself. Mrs. Allen disappoints her daughters' expectations for a new father by refusing to enter a marriage based upon misplaced love.

166. Grau, Shirley Ann. "Homecoming." The Wind Shifting West. New York: Alfred A. Knopf, 1973. 41 – 54.

A mother attempts to force her daughter into playing the role of a bereaved widow so that she can relive her own sorrow as a war widow in this story. Although Susan knew her classmate Harold only casually, her mother invites the whole neighborhood to mourn after the telegram arrives announcing his death in combat in Vietnam. This social occasion allows Susan's mother to relive the moment when her own husband was killed in action during the Korean War. When she was notified of the news of her husband's death in Korea, "the neighbors said you could hear her scream for a block; they found her huddled on the floor, stretched out flat and small as she could be with the bulging womb that held an almost completed baby named Susan" (44). But Susan has no comparable feelings toward Harold, even though she tries to invent them to please her mother and feels guilty at disappointing her because she has to honestly admit she has romantic feelings for Harold. The wake that Susan's mother carefully plans and orchestrates for Harold—even prescribing how her daughter should act while in mourning— is really a ceremony for herself as she imposes her own tragedy upon her daughter with expectations that never materialize because her daughter refuses to accept the role her mother has created for her.

167. Grau, Shirley Ann. "The Other Way." The Wind Shifting West. New York: Alfred A. Knopf, 1973. 148 – 154.

The black mother in this story pressures her daughter into remaining in an all-white school even though she is socially ostracized there. When the only other black student enrolled in school leaves, the remaining eight months of the school year stretch ahead for Sandra Lee "like the shining curve of a railroad track, endless" (153). " 'I don't belong there,' " Sandra Lee protests to her mother. " 'Where you belong, *chere* ?' " her mother snickers in retort. " 'You belong in Africa maybe? You going back to Africa wearing this dress?' " (152). The mother, whose withered legs have caused her to be dependent upon others all of her life, insists that her daughter continue in the all-white school so that she will not grow up to be a burden to others and will be able to compete in a white world. Sandra Lee's protests are silenced by her mother's directive: " 'You going back because there's no place else for you' " and her equally emphatic command to her daughter to never again complain about her unhappiness at school (152). Trapped in a all-white world at her mother's insistence, Sandra Lee faces a lonely adolescence in order to meet the expectations of a mother who offers little empathy or compassion for the loneliness she has placed upon her daughter.

168. Huffaker, Lucy. "The Way of Life." Atlantic Narratives. Ed. Charles Swain Thomas. Boston: Little, Brown, and Company, 1926. 145 – 158.

The mother of eight children in this story sacrifices the expectations she had for her daughter to become a great pianist when she allows her daughter to create her own dreams in this story. In the course of one evening Emmeline lives through her own childhood aspiration to become a musician and the shattering of her dreams with marriage and motherhood. Now a greater tragedy looms as her daughter chooses to marry and thus face the same possible loss of dreams. But Emmeline is comforted with the realization that dreams do last, even if fulfillment is impossible, and that her dreams will live on through her daughter, regardless of their outcome.

169. Hunter, Kristin. "Debut." Women and Men, Men and Women: An Anthology of Short Stories. Ed. William Smart. New York: St. Martin's Press, 1975. 8 – 14.

The black mother in this story concentrates so hard to prepare her adolescent daughter for the upward mobility she has never attained that she is unaware her only child is also learning the power of her emerging sexuality as a woman. Mrs. Simmons prepares her daughter for her first formal dance as if she were advancing to a battlefront. " 'It starts tonight,' " she informs her daughter, " 'and it goes on for the rest of your life. The battle to hold your head up and get someplace and be somebody. We've done all we can for you, your father and I. Now you've got to start fighting some on your own' " (9). Every detail of her daughter's appearance must be perfect. And it is. Judy surveys her reflection in the vanity mirror "as it it were a throne. She looked young and arrogant and beautiful and perfect and cold" (13). While Mrs. Simmons takes pride that her daughter has learned her lessons of social grace so adeptly, she is totally unaware that in the streets her daughter has also been gaining knowledge of herself as a woman. Judy has learned that her sexuality is a weapon that empowers her with a controlling influence over the men she meets, a potentially dangerous weapon in the hands of an inexperienced adolescent.

170. Johnson, Josephine W. "The Mother's Story." The Best American Short Stories 1951. Ed. Martha Foley. Boston: Houghton Mifflin, 1951. 157 – 167.

This story illustrates the emotional anguish a mother endures when her daughter's expectations for marriage are dashed by disappointment. "The Lord puts vile and grievous burdens on us all sometimes," the mother writes, "but He can break your heart quickest through a child" (162). Through the eyes of the mother who narrates this story, readers trace the relationship of her daughter to a young lawyer from infatuation to courtship to the patient expectation of a marriage proposal to devastating disappointment when the lawyer decides after months of prolonging the relationship and giving Laura false hopes that he favors his career more than marriage; there is not room for both in his life. The mother witnesses her once jubilant daughter paralyzed by a "dreadful demon" of anguish. "If you have ever seen a beautiful, happy child change through illness or torture and waste and age before your eyes into something like the white chrysalis of itself, then you will know and understand this spring," she writes somberly (165). Although Laura's condition gradually improves, she never fully recovers her passion for life and transforms into a different daughter than the one her mother has always known. Her mother writes with regrets:

> We lived peaceably and pleasantly together; but it was as though another and different child had come, and one we had to learn to know all over again. All the beautiful life you can't describe was gone. The sweetness was still there, but the light was out—the light that had made her seem a real miracle to us, and to everyone who knew her. (166)

This story poignantly expresses the agony of a mother who absorbs her daughter's sadness and grieves for her betrayal of love as she also grieves her own loss of her once radiant daughter.

171. Kincaid, Jamaica. "Girl." Sudden Fiction International: Sixty Short-Short Stories. Eds. Robert Shapard and James Thomas. New York: Norton, 1989. 65 – 66.

A mother's advice to her young black daughter offered in this short story (a two-page monologue comprised of one extended sentence) illustrates her own lack of self-esteem and the limited expectations she holds for her daughter's future. The maternal wisdom she passes on to her daughter takes the form of practical, life-sustaining skills a lower-class, self-sufficient woman needs to know in order to survive: how to cook pumpkin fritters, grow okra, sew a button, squeeze bread to insure it is fresh, "spit up in the air if you feel like it," bully men, avoid being a "slut" (although she expresses concern that her daughter's life seems to be moving in that direction), and abort an unwanted child. The life she envisions for her daughter, which can be inferred from their conversation, will be very much like her own, laden with monotonous manual labor, poverty, and unhappiness. There is no attempt on her part to build confidence in her daughter that she might overcome the unfortunate circumstances of her birthright; nor does she express any hope that her daughter might somehow escape the confines of poverty that have shaped her own existence.

172. Kohler, Sheila. "A Quiet Place." Miracles in America. New York: Alfred A. Knopf, 1990. 1990. 105 – 112.

The ambivalence of a young, unnamed mother (referred to in the story only as "the girl") toward motherhood is explored in this story. "The girl's" actions toward her two daughters reveal compassion as well as confining frustration with her role as mother. Motherhood is not as romantic as she envisioned it to be. "She had told all her school friends she would have six children, keep them all at home, and teach them herself. She would never send them to school. They would all run around and play games all day long" (109). But the labor and sacrifice of self involved in raising only two daughters is enough to try her patience, enough to cause her to dream that the younger, more demanding one is drowning and then wake in a frightened state of panic that perhaps her subconscious wish has come true. The extremes of emotions evoked by the motherhood experience, especially for a woman as young as "the girl" in this narrative who still clings to idealistic perceptions of mothering, are illustrated in this story.

173. Marshall, Lenore. "The Closed Door." The Confrontation and Other Stories. New York: W. W. Norton, 1972. 80 – 92.

The young daughter in this story discovers that her mother is not the perfect woman she has believed and come to expect her to be. The door between their rooms has always remained open, symbolizing the openness and closeness of their mother-daughter bond. But now the door has been closed for the first time, and no amount of denial can conceal the truth. Her mother is not only capable of committing adultery while her father is away on business, but she is equally capable of closing her adored daughter out of her life, if only temporarily. The emotionally painful recognition of her mother's very humanness also brings an opportunity for growth into this eight-year-old daughter's life, a simultaneous "strengthening and weakening." The closed door and shocking realization of her mother's adultery allows this daughter to view her mother as a less-than-perfect woman with needs and desires of her own and the right to occasionally close the door between them.

174. McCord, Jean. "I Left It All Behind When I Ran." Deep Where the Octopi Lie. New York: Atheneum, 1968. 85 – 98.

In this narrative a young woman anticipating leaving her rural home to enter art school learns that her mother, too, left home at the age of 16 to study art but failed to adjust to the frightening complexity of urban life and her own sudden independence. Her mother relates to her adolescent daughter the story of how she once left home to pursue the opportunity to become an artist but escaped back to the familiar before she had a chance to refine her talent and never drew again. But sometimes, she confesses to her daughter, she wonders what would have happened had she not run from the opportunity: "Just sometimes I wonder. What would have happened to me if I had stayed on to be an artist? Couldn't I have found out how to get by in that big city? I ponder and I wonder. I don't do my drawings no more. I left that all behind when I ran!" (97). Her daughter realizes as she now anticipates leaving home for the unknown ahead, feeling torn between the security of home and the yearning to be set free "like a caged wild bird," she carries with her the legacy of unfulfilled dreams her own mother once nourished. "She was asking me," the narrator writes, "to do something for her, to finish something that had started a long time ago" (98).

175. Naylor, Gloria. "Kiswana Browne." American Families: 28 Short Stories. Ed. Barbara H. Solomon. New York: New American Library, 1989. 219 – 232.

A black activist daughter clashes with her middle-class mother over her own future and the future of her race in this short narrative. It irritates Kiswana that her mother cannot accept her decision to change her name from Melanie to one that reflects her African heritage, her personal choice to live in a shabby neighborhood, her tiny apartment, her lack of employment—all attempts to establish her own independence. Most of all, her mother disapproves of her continued involvement in the black movement, which she views as wasted effort. The movement was important, she concedes to her daughter, " 'to stand up and say that you were proud of what you were and to get the vote and other social opportunities for every person in this country who had it due.' " " 'But,' " she reminds her daughter, " 'you kids thought you were going to turn the world upside down, and it just wasn't so. When all the smoke had cleared, you found yourself with a fistful of new federal laws and a country still full of obstacles for black people to fight their way over—just because they're black. There was no revolution, Melanie, and there will be no revolution' " (228). Instead of waiting for a revolution, she advises her daughter to fight within the system to foster racial reforms. Although Kiswana bitterly resents her mother's intrusions and attempts to direct her life, she realizes with reluctance and a bit of horror that her mother is right, that ultimately she will follow in her mother's footsteps and may even become the very person she most resents. Naylor effectively contrasts mother-daughter viewpoints toward racial heritage and reform in her fiction while she illustrates the strong maternal control that mothers exert over their daughters, even when their daughters try desperately but ineffectually to withstand this powerful influence.

176. Olsen, Tillie. "I Stand Here Ironing." Between Mothers and Daughters: Stories Across a Generation. Ed. Susan Koppelman. New York: The Feminist Press at the City University of New York, 1985. 178 – 187.

This monologue of a 38-year-old black mother dramatizes her fear that her oldest daughter's life will merely become an extension of her own poverty and disappointment. The conflict of the story, which won the O. Henry Memorial Prize Award as the best short story of 1961 and has been anthologized numerous times since, is not between mother and daughter but within the mother herself as she stands ironing, both envisioning and dreading the future for her 19-year-old daughter, hopeful that she will become "more than this dress on the ironing board, helpless before the iron," as she judges her own unproductive life to be (187). "Olsen's story," writes Helen Pike Bauer in "A child of anxious, not proud, love: Mother and Daughter in Tillie Olsen's 'I Stand Here Ironing,' " "is a dialogue between circumstances and desire, constraint and love, absence and presence, silence and speech, power and helplessness" (39). From two vantage points—reflection and projection—the mother reviews her own life's experiences (poverty, abandonment, single motherhood, monotonous labor, sickness) and hopes fervently that her daughter will escape a similar fate. The mother narrating her story expresses the hope that her daughter will develop a supportive "core of self-confidence, a sense of self-worth" that she never had, despite her underprivileged childhood. Although the mother-narrator wanted the best for her daughter as she was growing up, she was "so often forced to do the worst" because the maternal responsibilities and economic realities thrust upon her at an early age were too much to bear (178). "Even in the flinty world that this story traces," Bauer writes in her essay, "Olsen demonstrates enough faith in human resilience to hope that a daughter might find a better path than her mother trod"(39). In Tillie Olsen, Mickey Pearlman and Abby H. P. Werlock emphasize that neither mother nor daughter in this story succumb to the harsh circumstances of their lives as working mother and neglected daughter. These authors see significance in the fact that the mother's last act of the story is to control the iron. "Even if the iron has sometimes enslaved her," they write, "and even if she, the ironing mother, has sometimes unwittingly oppressed Emily with the way she has molded her life—both women emerge as survivors as well as victims" (62).

177. Prager, Emily. "A Visit From the Footbinder." Close Company: Stories of Mothers and Daughters. Eds. Christine Park and Caroline Heaton. New York: Ticknor and Fields, 1989. 48 – 76.

A Chinese empress continues the ancient tradition of footbinding in this narrative, ordering the painful procedure to be performed on her youngest daughter at the age of six so that her feet will "be as hummingbirds" and she will someday be an acceptable bride in society. Although Lady Guo Guo bound the feet of her first daughter, she pays a professional footbinder to perform the all-female ceremony for her second daughter, admitting, "It was worth it not to be the cause of pain" (75). As Pleasure Mouse forces her bound feet into shoes for the first time, her mother intones a prayer: " 'Oh, venerable ancestors, smile favourably upon my perky Pleasure Mouse, that she may marry well and one day see her own daughter's entry into womanhood. Take the first step, my child. Take the first step' " (72). Pleasure Mouse winces at her blood-soaked feet and collapses as she attempts her first step. It is then that she learns she will never be able to run again and will not walk without pain for at least two years, for she has paid the price of Chinese womanhood and met the expectations of her royal mother, who also shares her pain.

178. Schwartz, Lynne Sharon. "Over the Hill." Acquainted with the Night and Other Stories. New York: Harper and Row, 1984. 101 – 111.

Mother-daughter roles are reversed in this story when an adolescent daughter becomes offended by what she perceives as inappropriate social behavior for her single mother, whom she considers "over the hill" at age 34. Jealous over her mother's divided affection and attention, which she resents having to share with others, the daughter-narrator in this story takes it upon herself to try to diminish her mother's socializing and regain her sole attention, even to the point of lying to her mother's current lover. It is as if the respective roles of mother and daughter have been switched, the mother leading an active social life normally associated with a teenage girl while her adolescent daughter, serious beyond her 13 years, frowns unfavorably upon such frivolity like a disapproving mother, secretly nurturing the fear of losing the affection of the closest person in her life. Even though the narrator expresses confidence that her mother will once again reassure her that she is still the most important person in her life, she feels an obligation to force her childish mother into a serious adult role. "Because with kids it's different," the narrator explains, "I mean, that is why they're kids, but if grownups don't act their age who is going to keep any kind of order in the world?" (111). But it is not order this adolescent daughter really seeks, but the attention of a mother she deeply loves, even if she is clearly "over the hill."

179. Tan, Amy. "Two Kinds." Ed. Scott Walker. Stories from the American Mosaic. St. Paul: Graywolf Press, 1990. 188 – 201.

The daughter of a Chinese-American mother who immigrated to the United States believing "you could be anything you wanted to be in America" disappoints her mother by not becoming the child prodigy her mother anticipates in this story. While she is still young, the daughter-narrator believes her mother's expectations that she is destined for fame. She writes in retrospect:

> I pictured this prodigy part of me as many different images, trying each one on for size. I was a dainty ballerina girl standing by the curtains, waiting to hear the right music that would send me floating on my tiptoes. I was like the Christ Child lifted out of the straw manger, crying with holy indignity. I was Cinderella stepping from her pumpkin carriage with sparkly cartoon music filling the air.
>
> In all of my imaginings, I was filled with a sense that I would soon become *perfect*. (189)

After attempting several different endeavors, the narrator begins to realize it was not meant for her to become a child prodigy and defies her mother by refusing to practice the piano, for she knows she will never be a musical genius. " 'You want me to be someone that I'm not!' " she accuses her mother. " 'I'll never be the kind of daughter you want me to be.' " Her mother shouts back in Chinese that there are only two kinds of daughters—those who are obedient and those who demonstrate their own independence. In her home there is room for only one kind of daughter, she declares. " 'Obedient daughter!' " (198).

In her many failures, this daughter asserts her own will triumphantly—her "right to fall short of expectations." Unlike my mother, she writes, "I did not believe I could be anything I wanted to be. I could only be me" (199). Her assertion of individuality and rejection of her mother's continual pressure for perfection lead to a more contented sense of self-worth and independence in this daughter.

180. Whittier, Gayle. "Turning Out." Fiction of the Eighties: a decade of stories from TriQuarterly. Eds. Reginald Gibbons and Susan Hahn. Chicago: Northwestern University, 1990. 213 – 232.

The daughter in this narrative must not only face her own failure as a ballet dancer—while her best friend excels at the art—but the disappointment of her mother as well whose expectations of an ideal daughter "alive only in her dangerous maternal mind" have been crushed by disappointment. While the already tall daughter of 14 years envisions herself continuing to grow each year into a "dancing giantess of eighteen, demoted, year by year, from the Ballet Russe to the sideshow," her mother continues to coach from the sidelines in hopes that her daughter's mediocre talent will miraculously bloom into perfection. When Bonnie overhears her mother discussing with her father the possibility of having another child, she must also cope with the devastating truth that she could be replaced in her mother's affections by a more talented sister who might be able to fulfill her mother's dreams and expectations for a perfect ballerina.

181. Williams, Shirley A. (as S. A. Williams). "Tell Martha Not to Moan." Out of Our Lives: A Selection of Contemporary Black Fiction. Ed. Quandra Prettyman Stadler. Washington, DC: Howard University Press, 1975. 114 – 134.

The black mother and daughter in this story come into conflict because Martha chooses not to follow in the footsteps of her Biblical namesake and meet the expectations set by her mother. When she becomes pregnant for the second time with no plans for marriage or financial support from her musician lover, her mother advises her to end the relationship. " 'Martha,' " she tells her daughter, " 'I named you after that woman in the Bible cause I want you to be like her. Be good in the same way she is. Martha, that woman ain't never stopped believing. She humble and patient and the Lord make a place for her' " (133 – 134). But Martha ignores the words (and expectations) of her mother, choosing instead to listen to the dubious promises of her lover repeating themselves over and over in her mind: " 'You feel good . . . You gon be my Black queen? . . . We can make it together . . . You feel good . . .' " (134).

182. Wisenberg, S. L. "Pageant." My Mother's Daughter: Stories by Women. Ed. Irene Zahava. Freedom, CA: The Crossing Press, 1991. 143 – 150.

The reactions of an eight-year-old daughter pressured by her mother to perform oral interpretations during talent competitions are examined in this story. When Ceci fails to take first place in a contest, her grandparents offer her flowers with sympathy and words of encouragement, but her mother is less forgiving, lashing out at her daughter in frustration with "sharp surprise cracks of real pain" that sting and pop and make her daughter wish that her mother would die. Although she enters more competitions, reciting the memoirs of Eleanor Roosevelt and Helen Keller her mother has chosen for the occasion, Ceci is judged as a finalist less and less. She remembers the afternoon of the competition that ended in her mother striking her "as not the end of her childhood or of anything hallowed like innocence but the day she realized that no one understood her, no one would ever understand her, the day she felt her heart begin to close" (150). Her most ardent desire becomes to escape from this life where even something as basic as maternal acceptance is unpredictable and often denied.

Sources:

Bauer, Helen Pike. "A child of anxious, not proud, love: Mother and Daughter in Tillie Olsen's 'I Stand Here Ironing.' " Mother Puzzles: Daughters and Mothers in Contemporary American Literature. Ed. Mickey Pearlman. Westport, CT: Greenwood Press, 1989. 35 – 39.

Kannenstine, Louis F. The Art of Djuna Barnes: Duality and Damnation. New York: New York University Press, 1977.

Pearlman, Mickey and Abby H. P. Werlock. Tillie Olsen. Boston: Twayne Publishers, 1991.

6

Nurturance

INTRODUCTION

The importance of maternal acceptance, support, and nurturance from the time of infant bonding through adulthood is illustrated by the stories in this chapter. Daughters who know the security of maternal love are empowered with a special confidence that can sustain them through the inevitable adversities of life. Mothers and daughters characterized in several of these stories attain a closeness that resembles woman to woman friendship more than kinship.

The nurturing instinct that mothers naturally possess for their infant daughters is illustrated in stories written by Susan Engberg and Joyce Carol Oates. The mother in Engberg's "Household" remembers when she first viewed her newborn daughter shortly after birth, she marveled that she carried both fetus and umbilical cord as well as a wealth of sudden maternal emotions inside of her body. "There couldn't have been space for all of that, she had felt, and what had been set in motion seemed then, as now, larger than she had known she had room for" (209). The heart of the new mother in Oates's "A Touch of the Flu" swells with "love, exaltation, greed" as she strolls with her young daughter along a New England seashore, introducing her to many natural wonders of the world which have been created anew in her vision by their "delicious union" as mother and daughter. "Sand, ocean, butterly, cloud, sky, do you see?" she asks. "Wind, sun—do you feel?" (64)

The sensual nature of the mother-daughter relationship is illustrated in stories written by Sara Vogan and Audre Lorde. Young daughters in these stories are introduced early during their childhoods to the senual nature of womanhood through intimate contact with their mothers. The mother in Rachel Simon's "Breath of This Night" attempts to capture and preserve the essence of her three young daughters. As each daughter breathes into a jar, her mother carefully labels the jar with her name, anticipating the time far into the future when she will open the jar and savor the special essence of each of her daughters. The rich imaginations of a mother and her young daughter in Helen Schulman's "Not a Free Show" allow them to rise above the "crushingly dull" routine of small town life as they create a rich fantasy world of their own.

Narratives written by Helen Schulman and Jamaica Kincaid illustrate how intensely close the mother-daughter relationship can become. Even after the daughters in their stories approach adulthood and begin to move toward independence, they remain closely entwined in the mother-daughter bond. "I do not know where I end and she begins again," admits the daughter in Schulman's "Not a Free Show." "When something happens for me, it is like it happens for her. When things go rotten, I feel guilty, when I am upset I ruin her life. On the other hand, when things go well, I rejoice her" (143). She cannot begin to imagine what her life would be like if she were to outlive her mother. " 'I don't know how to live without her,' " she confesses. " 'For me she is intrinsic. I cannot survive her. I cannot survive my mother' " (144). As mother and daughter walk together in Kincaid's "My Mother," their steps and voices seem to blend into one. "What peace came over me then," writes the daughter-narrator, "for I could not see where she left off and I began, or where I left off and she began" (97).

Despite her poverty and simple lifestyle the mother in Shirley Ann Grau's "The Beginning" empowers her young daughter with the hope of infinite possibility. By the time the narrator of the story discovers she is an illegitimate black woman instead of a chosen princess, she is beyond vulnerability because her life has been built on such a strong foundation of love and security, carefully constructed by a caring mother. In contrast, the single black mother in Cheryl Ann Alexander's "Exile" can only share the sorrow and rejection of her adolescent daughter whose poverty and mixed blood have branded her a social outcast in New York City.

The mothers and daughters in stories written by Jill Ciment, Kathleen Coskran, and Linda Hogan are bonded in mutual hopelessness in their poverty, yet the strength of their bonds of love help them survive the adverse circumstances they face. Although the Native-American mother in Hogan's "New Shoes" wears shoes that are worn and scuffed, she rejoices as much as her pre-adolescent daughter when her own sacrifices enable her to purchase her daughter's first pair of black patent leather shoes.

The mother and daughter in Marilyn Krysl's "Mother and Child" bond together in joint resistance against male violence in this post-World War Two story. The mother vows to fill her young daughter with her own abundant reservoir of peaceful energy so that together they may rise above the destructive force of male violence.

A mother and daughter celebrate the advent of the daughter's first mentrual cycle as yet another symbol of their common bond as women in Susan Neville's "Rain Forest" while the mother in Bobbie Ann Mason's "Marita" guides her daughter through the trauma of an abortion. Roxana Robinson's narrative "Daughter" explores the fragile delineation between maternal nurturance and overprotection. Although the mother in this story is admittedly and uncontrollably "profligate with my affection, extravagant with my love for my daughter," she is concerned that her excessive love might inhibit her young daughter's ability to individuate (114). The mother-narrator is relieved when she sees signs of independence emerging in her young daughter as she leaves for school. "Perhaps she will escape me after all," the mother sighs hopefully (117).

It is the daughters who are the nurturers of their mothers in short fictions written by Frances Sherwood and Nancy Richard. Daughters in these stories show compassionate concern for their mother's needs in a reversal of roles based upon love and unexpected circumstances. In Annette

Sanford's "Girls in the Garden" it is the grandmother who becomes the surrogate mother and primary nurturer of her granddaughters while their own mother rejects motherhood, at least for the time being, as she attempts to find herself.

SHORT FICTION

183. Alexander, Cheryl Ann. "Exile." The Things That Divide Us. Eds. Faith Conlon, Rachel da Silva, and Barbara Wilson. Seattle: Seal Press, 1985.

The single black mother in this narrative shares the sorrow and rejection of her adolescent daughter whose poverty and mixed blood brand her a social outcast at a time in her life when friendships and acceptance are of greatest importance. Although Anne is intelligent and accepted by classmates during school hours, their friendship ends at the end of the school day when Anne returns to her Harlem residence, a victim of an "invisible color barrier." Her mother not only shares her aloneness but feels a strong sense of maternal guilt for moving to New York City instead of remaining in Trinidad, Anne's birthplace, where her daughter might have grown up in an environment where she would be more socially accepted.

184. Ascher, Carol. "Remembering Berlin—1979." My Mother's Daughter: Stories by Women. Ed. Irene Zahava. Freedom, CA: The Crossing Press, 1991. 172 – 188.

A mother and daughter explore the mother's past in this story as they return together to Berlin where the mother was evacuated "into the unknown" for her protection by her parents forty years earlier when World War Two began. Mother and daughter visit the places that illustrate the mother's "wonderful stories of her enchanted childhood as the loved youngest daughter of a large prosperous family, fairy tales that turned by sister's and my Kansas childhood dull," the daughter writes (172). These same adventurous stories, however, instilled fear in the daughter-narrator who remembers living in "constant dread of losing everything I loved in some unknown holocaust." She remembers a recurring nightmare: "I would walk among the rubble of a totally destroyed city, the lone survivor. For years I had waited for this disaster" (172). Now as mother and daughter safely explore the city that cultivated such fantasies and fears, the daughter realizes the importance of this "beloved city" which her mother can now only believe herself to be a part of in her imagination.

185. Braverman, Kate. "These Clairvoyant Ruins." Squandering the Blue. New York: Fawcett Columbine, 1990. 225 – 241.

A mother facing the age of 41, trying to sort out her own life and identity, forgives her eight-year-old daughter for accusing her of being a bad mother in this story. Although she has committed the parental sin of forgetting to play the tooth fairy and has insisted that her daughter continue violin lessons when Annabel protests "the chic thing is piano," Diana looks beyond the immediacy of her young daughter's fickleness and self-centeredness to the larger questions of life and death which loom at middle age and finds at least some of the answers in the darkness. "It is in the ruins of this darkness that we absolve the ones who love us badly," she writes. "In the darkness where we know ourselves absolutely and we are fueled by ancient griefs and luminous without stars" (241).

186. Ciment, Jill. "Astronomy." Small Claims. New York: Weidenfeld and Nicolson, 1986. 13 – 24.

A daughter and her single mother both come to accept their own powerlessness in the scope of the universe in this story. While the mother seeks to change her identity (and hopefully her fate) with a different hair color each week, her daughter fails at her first business venture attempted to pay the electricity bill. The daughter comes to view herself as hopeless as the insect she watches Johny Swat sail into orbit from the top of a golf ball. " 'Mom, we're no different from insects,' " she tells her mother. " 'You're telling me,' " the mother agrees (24). When the mother eventually runs out of new hairstyles and cuts off all of her hair so that her daughter can "see me for what I am," the daughter admits that her mother may not "look too good now, but she thought she was beautiful" (24).

187. Coskran, Kathleen. "The High Price of Everything." The High Price of Everything. St. Paul: New Rivers Press, 1988. 1 – 14.

The entrapment of poverty frustrates the Georgian mother and daughter in this story as the mother realizes her daughter is becoming an adolescent and needs the clothes of a woman instead of those of a child, but she cannot afford to purchase them. While the mother publicly berates her daughter for asking for larger clothes to replace those she has outgrown, in private the narrator overhears her mother begging her father in vain for a credit card so that she can purchase suitable clothes for her daughter. Although the mother in this story doesn't allow her daughter to know her feelings, she shares with her daughter the pain of her entering womanhood with only the purchase of one blue skirt "that will go with everything" and bargain basement panties.

188. Engberg, Susan. "Household." A Stay By the River. New York: Viking, 1985. 183 – 210.

The 41-year-old mother in this story nurtures her own newborn daughter as she struggles with the adjustments and demands of first time motherhood even as she plays the role of surrogate mother to the daughter of a childhood friend seeking temporary solace from the outside world. At times Nathalie is awed by the wonders of motherhood:

> When the baby had been newly born, she had been placed for a few moments on Nathalie's abdomen and, feeling the new weight, Nathalie had raised her head and marveled with some shock that this complete and thrusting creature, still umbilically connected but now with a once-vital layer of nature's protection withdrawn, had actually been carried inside her body; there couldn't have been space for all of that, she had felt, and what had been set in motion seemed then, as now, larger than she had known she had room for. (209)

At other times Nathalie feels completely overwhelmed by the demands that motherhood has made upon her time, patience, interrupted career, and privacy, especially when she finds herself unexpectedly attempting to mother two daughters with very different needs at the same time, "a newborn infant and an infantile twenty-one-year-old; what a combination" (186).

189. Grau, Shirley Ann. "The Beginning." Nine Women. New York: Alfred A. Knopf, 1985. 5 – 17.

This story is a tribute to mothers who are able to empower their daughters with a sense of self-respect and infinite possibility despite the circumstances of their birth. The mother in this narrative showers her young daughter with love and security, convincing her at an early age that she is the "queen of the world, the jewel of the lotus, the pearl without price, my secret treasure" (5). Although she and her mother, a single parent, live a simple existence and are forced to move often during the narrator's childhood until the mother eventually establishes her own dresssmaking business, the welfare and self-esteem of her daughter are always the first concern of this caring mother, who assures her daughter she is a princess worthy of all the amenities linked to such a title. By the time the young princess discovers the truth of her lineage, she is beyond vulnerability because she has such a strong foundation of love and security. As an adult the narrator writes retrospectively of her past:

> And so I passed my childhood disguised to myself as a princess. I thrived, grew strong and resilient. When the kingdom at last fell and the castle was conquered, and I lost my crown and my birthright, when I stood naked and revealed as a young black female of illegitimate birth, it hardly mattered. By then the castle and the kindgom were within me and I carried them away. (17)

190. Hogan, Linda. "New Shoes." Earth Power Coming: Short Fiction in Native American Literature. Ed. Simon J. Ortiz. Tsaile, AZ: Navajo Community College Press, 1983. 3 – 20.

A Native American mother grieves for the urban life she and her pre-adolescent daughter must lead while she shares her daughter's joy as she dons her first pair of grownup shoes in this story. Sullie knows that a mother working as a motel maid and daughter living alone in the city is "no good," not the life she would envision for her half-Indian daughter. Donna's childhood memories will contain "no wide open spaces, no sounds of lake water touching up against the sores in a slow rhythm like maybe it loved the land" as she remembers from her own childhood. Donna is growing up in an entirely different culture. "Like a stranger. She was going to be a white girl. Sullie could already see it in her" (10). Although their future looks bleak and Sullie wears shoes that are "flat and worn, scuffed," she manages to save enough to purchase her daughter her first grownup pair of shoes. Sullie shares her daughter's anticipation of womanhood and initial realization that she is an attractive female as Donna surveys her image in the mirror wearing her first pair of black patent leather shoes.

191. Kincaid, Jamaica. "My Mother." Close Company: Stories of Mothers and Daughters. New York: Ticknor and Fields, 1989. 93 – 98.

The nine vignettes of fantasy that comprise this imagery-rich narrative trace the evolution of a mother-daughter relationship through several stages of merging and separating as the daughter matures from a child to a woman, trying to reconcile her dependency upon her mother with her need for individuation. The narrator feels the most contentment in her relationship with her mother when the two of them walk and talk together, their steps and voices blending into one. "What peace came over me then," she writes, "for I could not see where she left off and I began, or where I left off and she began" (97).

192. Krysl, Marilyn. "Mother and Child." Mozart, Westmoreland, and Me. New York: Thunder's Mouth Press, 1985. 85 – 93.

A mother and her young daughter bond together in joint resistance to the forces of male violence that seem to surround their lives in this story. Although World War Two is technically three years past, Ethel sees evidence within her own family that the violence perpetuated by men against one another continues. President Harry Truman proclaims over the radio that " 'America is still the toughest country in the world today' " (91). And men continue to prove their toughness, charging each other "like mad bulls," Ethel observes:

> They thought of life as a battle. Other men were the enemies, life was a contest, and pride insisted you fight. They would fight over the most casual remark as though the reputation of a whole country hung in the balance, as though they thought themselves as important as nations. The war wasn't over at all, it simply continued as though men had to have it to do, as though they couldn't stop. (92)

Although Ethel tries to rationalize the behavior of the men in their lives to her young daughter, she knows she does not believe her own words. There are no explanations for male brutality. And women, even though who try to escape, are often swept involuntarily into the midst of violence because they cannot get away. These women, like Ethel, suffer the consequences of male violence even though they have done nothing to perpetuate it.

It is the sight of her young daughter's radiance and innocence which prevents Ethel from sinking into total despair. Her anger at the senselessness of male violence and her own powerlessness to stop it dissolves into a liquid, only to expand and rise again as a billowing burst of energy. "This good substance was hers and she had plenty of it, she embodied it, it rose in her, propelling her. It was hers, it would not go away" (92). She vows to fill her daughter with this "lightness, infuse her with airiness, plump her up, blow on her gently like you blew on a hurt bird to encourage it to fly," so that together they will not succumb to the destruction of male violence but to rise above it (93).

193. Lorde, Audre. "How I Became a Poet." My Mother's Daughter: Stories by Women. Ed. Irene Zahava. Freedom, CA: The Crossing Press, 1991. 104 – 108.

Reflections of a daughter's initial, sensual relationship with her mother are remembered in this story. "*I am a reflection of my mother's secret poetry as well as of her hidden angers*," writes the daughter-narrator. "I remember the warm mother smell caught between her legs, and intimacy of our physical touching nestled inside of the anxiety/pain like a nutmeg nestled inside its covering of mace" (106). The poet traces her own gift of words to her mother's "special and secret relationship with words" she observed as she was growing up in her mother's inspirational presence.

194. Mason, Bobbie Ann. "Marita." Mother Jones. May 1988: 41 – 46.

A mother nurtures her daughter through an abortion and helps her redirect her life in this story, narrated in part by the daughter and partially by an omniscient narrator. When Marita's mother realizes her daughter is pregnant, she convinces her to have an abortion and return to college, rather than give birth to a child which she will undoubtedly lose interest in and depend upon her mother to raise. Marita realizes that her mother's advice represents wisdom she wishes she had followed 18 years ago when she found herself unwed and pregnant. Fearing that her daughter will follow a life pattern similar to her own, marrying too young without the "chance to see a Broadway show or go backpacking," she supports her daughter as she undergoes an abortion. Following the procedure, mother and daughter make plans for Marita to return to college and continue her life, as planned.

195. Naslund, Sena Jeter. "Ice Skating at the North Pole." Ice Skating at the North Pole. Bristol, RI: Ampersand Press, 1989. 23 – 37.

The mother who narrates this story attempts to pass on to her daughter a legacy of strength and security she derived from her own mother. "I look at my empty hands and into them, and I see my mother's bones," the narrator writes. "I have always had a special strength because I have always known that my own mother would do anything for me" (25). During childhood the narrator remembers her mother saved her from the threat of wild animals and fire and fashioned sturdy cotton belts in their automobile long before seat belts were invented. She names her own daughter Rosetta, after her mother, Rose. Even as she sees evidence that her marriage is failing, the narrator seeks to protect Rose as she was protected so that she may be "safe as a child swaddled in a good marriage" (37). When her daughter begs to ice skate on a nearby pond one wintry day, the narrator immediately envisions the possible dangers of this reckless suggestion, a crack in the ice opening like a "black mouth," her daughter sinking into the freezing water, flinging her arms in hysteria for her mother to save her. But in her mind she immediately replaces this grim vision with a safer fantasy in which she and her daughter travel north by dog sled until at last the needle of the compass points straight down. "Here there is never wind," the mother writes. "At our feet, the wind has blown the ice clear of snow, a perfect lens. Like the eye of a hurricane, this place is the eye of the world" (37). Here, the narrator knows her daughter may skate in safety, for "I know this ice is a mile thick, has never been known to thaw," she ends the narrative (37).

196. Neville, Susan. "Rain Forest." The Invention of Flight. Athens: University of Georgia Press, 1984. 72 – 80.

A mother and daughter grow closer in their common womanhood in this story as the nine-year-old daughter begins her first menstrual period and tries to understand the "warmth or a rumbling of something happening in a part of her body she'd always thought was her stomach" (72). The "animal" she senses growing within represents a transition from childhood to adulthood and prompts both physical and mental changes. As their similiarities as women become more obvious, the daughter begins to build a closer identification with her mother.

197. Oates, Joyce Carol. "A Touch of the Flu." My Mother's Daughter: Stories by Women. Ed. Irene Zahava. Freedom, CA: The Crossing Press, 1991. 63 – 64.

A woman's ambivalent feelings toward motherhood are illustrated in this short narrative. The mother is characterized as a woman so full of love for her daughter that she has none left for the child's father. She cherishes the opportunity to nurture her young daughter and introduce her to the wonders of the vast world that seem "newly created" in her mind by their "delicious union" as mother and daughter. Exploring a New England seashore together, "she held her little girl in her arms, aloft, in triumph, her heart swelling with love, exaltation, greed. Sand, ocean, butterfly, cloud, sky, do you see? Wind, sun—do you feel?" (64)

But the intensity of motherhood can also be overwhelming, Oates's story illustrates. During a visit to her parents' home, the mother suddenly give up her daughter to the care of her own mother, if only temporarily, to offer herself the opportunity to retreat from mothering and find solace alone.

198. Owens, Michele. "We Find Harris Again." Hot Type: America's Most Celebrated Writers Introduce the Next Word in Contemporary Fiction. Ed. John Miller. New York: Macmillan, 1988. 127 – 145.

The mother who narrates this story guides and supports her daughter through unexpected motherhood and a renewed relationship with the father of her child. "My feeling for my daughter is a constant struggle between empathy and concern," the mother-narrator confesses. Characterized as a woman who is as much a friend as a mother, the mother, described in Mona Simpson's introduction to the story as a "guarded romantic, with endless capacities for generosity and expansion," accepts her daughter's ambivalence about marriage and motherhood without interference or intrusion (128).

199. Poliner, Elizabeth. "Swimming like an Eel." Iowa Woman. Autumn 1990: 35 – 41.

An adolescent daughter accepts her mother's affair in this story and urges her mother to divorce her father for her own happiness. More like friends than mother and daughter, the female characters in this story enjoy a close relationship that contrasts with the strained, distant relationship of the parents. While the mother speaks frankly of her unhappiness and attraction to other men, the narrator reassures her that a divorce is the best alternative as she, too, experiences a sense of freedom with the finality of her mother's decision.

200. Richard, Nancy. "Annie, Listening." Something in Common: Contemporary Louisiana Stories. Ed. Ann Brewster Dobie. Baton Rouge: Louisiana State University Press, 1991. 265 – 277.

It is the 12-year-old daughter-narrator of this story who becomes the nurturer of her mentally ill mother. During the mother's disappearance (she leaves her children a note confessing that she cannot live with them anymore) and subsequent hospitalization, the narrator comes to understand how her mother perceives life. Although her mother may be persuaded to return home, she will always feel deficient as a mother. " 'I'm sorry,' " she apologizes to her daughter, " 'I don't know how to be your mother. I keep getting it wrong' " (275). The daughter-narrator learns to accept that no matter what she does or promises to do, she is powerless to make life easier for her mother to bear. The daughter also develops a maternal protectiveness toward her mother (exemplified by such actions as not allowing herself to sleep until she is assured her mother has fallen asleep first) and a respect for her fragile mental state.

201. Robinson, Roxana. "Daughter." A Glimpse of Scarlet and Other Stories. New York: Edward Burlingame Books, 1991. 112 – 117.

The conflicting desires of an admittedly overprotective mother to continue to foster intimacy with her five-year-old daughter yet allow her to individuate are expressed by the mother-narrator of this story. "I appear to be a kind and generous mother," the narrator writes. "I am profligate with my affection, extravagant with my love for my daughter. I read to her for hours, I give her milk and graham crackers after school, we have long talks, expeditions, but she and I know the intensity of the demands I make on her. I want her simply perfect: modeled after me but without my flaws" (114). Although the mother prolongs their parting in the morning with shared intimacies and assurances of affection, she is relieved to see that tangible signs of independence are emerging in her young daughter as she departs for school: "Perhaps she will escape me after all," the mother sighs hopefully (117).

202. Sanford, Annette. "Girls in the Garden." Lasting Attachments. Dallas: Southern Methodist University Press, 1989. 13 – 24.

A grandmother assumes the nurturing role of mother for her two preadolescent granddaughters in this story of maternal rejection and surrogate acceptance. The adult daughter, a restaurant hostess and aspiring model, advises her daughters "to decide what is most productive and put that first" (14). It is not her daughters who are the first priority in her life. While she lives with her latest lover in a condominium that includes a sauna and maid service but prohibits children, her daughters "lead the quiet life" with their grandmother, playing Parcheesi and making grocery lists on the backs of old envelopes. "On cold nights we dress in our nightgowns right after supper," writes the daughter-narrator. "We eat popcorn and Mam takes down her hair and reads to me out of books with the covers falling off" (17).

The narrator confides to her grandmother that she hopes her mother lives "for a long time in a place where the management doesn't allow children" (24). Wrapping her in maternal warmth and security, her grandmother assures her there is no need to worry.

203. Schmidt, Heidi Jon. "The Art of Conversation." The Rose Thieves. New York: Harcourt Brace Jovanovich, 1990. 1 – 8.

A mother and her young daughter rise above the "crushingly dull" routine of small town life in this story, using books and their imaginations to create a wonderfully varied and rich fantasy world of their own. When the daughter fails in her first attempts to make polite conversation with adults, she realizes with delight that she will never be able to speak the language of "common life" she finds "strange and wonderful" but out of reach. For she and her mother have become allies against the mundane, bonded by their mutual disdain for the ordinary, their impatience with anything practical, and their shared fascination with the extraordinary.

204. Schulman, Helen. "Not a Free Show." Not a Free Show. New York: Alfred A. Knopf, 1988. 130 – 144.

This series of vignettes traces the evolution of a young woman and her relationship with her mother from the year the narrator is three (her first memory is of her mother's sadness over the assassination of John Fitzgerald Kennedy) until early adulthood. The narrative traces their relationship through peace marches, childhood diseases, pet funerals, ballet lessons, and teenage birth control, deaths, and college. As the daughter matures and alternately moves toward independence and then back again to the loving security of her mother's nurturance, she realizes that, despite their separate identities, she and her mother have become entwined beings. "I do not know where I end and she begins again," the daughter admits. "When something happens for me, it is like it happens for her. When things go rotten, I feel guilty, when I am upset I ruin her life. On the other hand, when things go well, I rejoice her" (143). When a lover asks how the daughter plans to survive when her mother eventually dies, she answers in desperation and need, " 'I don't know. I don't know how to live without her. For me she is intrinsic. I cannot survive her. I cannot survive my mother' " (144).

205. Schwartz, Lynne Sharon. "What I Did For Love." The Melting Pot and Other Subversive Stories. New York: Harper and Row, 1987. 110 – 130.

A mother with admittedly no genuine affinity for guinea pigs arranges for emergency eye surgery and follows an extensive regimen of post-op care to save the life of her daughter's pet in this story of maternal devotion. The mother-narrator confesses she has never especially liked guinea pigs, but when the life of her daughter's fourth rodent in four years is threatened while she is away at camp, the mother pays $75 for emegency surgery which leaves Rudy one-eyed and follows a complicated procedure to insure that his wound heals. As the narrator counts down the days until her daughter's return, she nurses the pet with maternal devotion. "So I'm applying the warm compresses for the last time," she writes, "sitting here with a one-eyed guinea pig who is going to live out his four-to-six-year life span no matter what it takes, in the middle of the journey of my life, stroking him as if I really loved animals" (130).

206. Sherwood, Frances. "Lessons in Love: A Memoir." Everything You've Heard is True. Baltimore: Johns Hopkins University Press, 1989. 34 – 42.

This sketch portrays a 36-year-old mother and her adolescent daughter, who share a bond of mutual rejection in romantic love. Born of "pioneer stock," the narrator's mother encourages her daughter not to be afraid to "take the world on, it's all yours." But the narrator's plans to leave behind the "inarticulate country people" of Nebraska and live with her boyfriend as "avant-garde bohemians" collapse when he is accepted at MIT while she is rejected at Radcliffe. When her mother, too, feels the sting of rejection from her current lover, the narrator searches for something to say to ease that familiar pain. She writes:

> I wondered what comfort I could offer as we sat across from each other with two white plates in front of us, napkins folded, silverware at attention, glasses turned down against any free-floating germ. We were stranded there, marooned on a green oilcloth in a checkerboard sea of linoleum where once flying flapjacks had cavorted. (42)

It is her empathy and understanding that this daughter can best offer to her mother as they both begin to recover from similar emotional losses.

207. Simon, Rachel. "Breath of This Night." Little Nightmares, Little Dreams. Boston: Houghton Mifflin, 1990. 15 – 20.

A mother seeks to preserve the memory of her three young daughters so that she can forever savor the essence of each of them as she grows old in this story. Each daughter carefully breathes her own breath into a jar as her mother captures her special essence and carefully labels the jar with her name. " 'Everyone's breath is special because it only comes once, and then it's gone,' " she explains to her daughters. " 'It's like taking a picture, except you can't see what it looks like' " (19). Lining the jars along the headboard of her bed, the mother-narrator envisions the day when she becomes a widowed grandmother, carefully opening the lid of each jar. She writes:

> I'll turn the lids slowly, and sniff the contents like fine wines. I'll put my face into each jar, as deep as the opening will allow, and breathe in my children's breath. And I will remember this night. Suspended for long, then lost in an instant. So much, I'll think then, like flower under glass, crumbling into dust when its petals touch the air. (20)

208. Simon, Rachel, "Launching the Echo." Little Nightmares, Little Dreams. Boston: Houghton Mifflin, 1990. 139 – 145.

A mother shares a special moment with her three young daughters in this story while she releases her frustrations at all males after experiencing several failed relationships with men. Standing on the edge of a cliff during a family trip, awed by the scenery surrounding them, the daughters are captivated when they discover the echoing sounds of their voices in the valley below. When the daughters demand that their mother shout something, she automatically responds by focusing all of her anger into one word, as she wails angrily: " 'Mmmmm—en.' " Soon the mother and her three daughters are shouting the same " 'Mmmmm—en,' " their voices filling the valley. "I look at them and notice their huge grins and how this shouting together makes them jump up and down," the mother-narrator writes. "Someday my girls will have their own histories with men. I wonder if this memory will make them smile then" (145).

209. Simon, Rachel. "The Long Sadness of No." Little Nightmares, Little Dreams. Boston: Houghton Mifflin, 1990. 107 – 111.

The daughter who narrates this story shares her mother's grief for having loved a man with multiple sclerosis she could not marry and for having married a man she did not love. The daughter grows up balancing her mother's romantic stories of her love for Peter with the reality that their relationship could not last. As an adult, the daughter dreams a tragic nightmare in which Peter and her mother are almost united. But she spares her 60-year-old mother, who has survived a series of failed relationships with men since Peter, the details of the dream. "It would only be cruel," she realizes. "Life is hard enough without your children tugging at your sleeve, bringing up things that cannot be changed" (111).

210. Tetu, Randeane. "The Map." Merle's & Marilyn's Mink Ranch. Watsonville, CA: Papier-Mache Press, 1991. 58 – 63.

A mother and daughter make plans for what course of action they will take should a nearby power plant explode in this story, but it is the daughter who plans to escape while the mother determines she will stay in her own house regardless of the potential danger to come. While she urges her daughter to make preparations to evacuate should the explosion occur, the mother insists that she will stay in her own home, telling her daughter: " 'I would sit in this chair with my knitting on my lap—you make sure I can reach my knitting that's all I ask—and I'll sit here and let radiation creep around me—through me. I don't mind. I hope it's quick' " (58). Even as she sets aside her own fears of dying, the mother worries for the safety of her daughter, fearful that she will not be able to evacuate in time. While mother and daughter plan detailed strategies should such a disaster occur, each respects the individual choices of the other, the mother opting to remain in her own home until she dies while the daughter plans to flee for her safety.

211. Thurm, Marian. "Romance." These Things Happen. New York: Poseidon Press, 1988. 121 – 137.

The mother and daughter characterized in this story are so entwined in their own love and friendship that an interested suitor cannot penetrate the barrier of closeness that unites them. The mother and daughter, both divorcees, share an apartment and interact more like devoted sisters than mother and daughter. Their relationship baffles Ross, who assumes that all mother-daughter relationships resemble his mother and sister's—a long series of disagreements and disappointments.

Although the mother and daughter characterized in this story are both obviously fond of Russ's company, he cannot feel more than the "loneliness of an intruder" into their relationship, solidified by an impenetrable mother-daughter bond that happily unites these self-sufficient women who seemingly have no need for men in their lives.

212. Vogan, Sara. "Mozart in the Afternoon." Scenes from the Homefront. Chicago: University of Illinois Press, 1987. 117 – 123.

The adult daughter who narrates this story recalls long, hot, summer afternoons of sensual pleasure spent bathing with her mother while they sipped cool fruit drinks and listened to classical music. The daughter remembers being introduced to the pleasures of combining vodka and Mozart, gin and Bach, and erotica and orgasm during these special mother-daughter afternoons.

7

Portraits

INTRODUCTION

A sweatshop worker who labors over a sewing machine all day to provide for her four children. A trapeze artist who informs her daughter that she'd be "amazed at how many things a person can do within the act of falling" (234). A "driving woman" who raises 11 children by herself when her husband responds to a vision that tells him to move into a nearby shed with his dog. A mother who makes a habit of sneaking her four children to the movie theater in their pajamas late at night so that she can enjoy the late-night features. These are examples of the diversity of women characterized in the stories of this chapter, all of whom have at least one trait in common—they are all mothers who have given birth to daughters. And many of their stories are narrated by the daughters themselves.

Stories written by Kate Braverman, Wanda Coleman, and Shirley Ann Grau are portraits of poverty in which daughter-narrators describe how their single mothers struggle to support their families. These women have little energy left to be mothers after their exhausting days at work have ended. A typical mother portrayed in this chapter is the sweatshop worker in Wanda Coleman's "The Seamstress" who labors over a sewing machine eight hours daily to support her family. Despite her fatigue at day's end, she finds reserves of energy left to finish sewing a new dress for her 11-year-old daughter at night. "I wonder as a I watch her," the narrator writes of her mother and her labor with a mixture of pride and curiosity. "What must it be like? And what makes her battle it so hard and never give in?" (40).

Many of the mothers in these stories are portrayed as women in search of themselves as they resolve mid-life crises. The mother in Sally Benson's "Birds in Their Nests Agree" finds her life overtaken by a "deadly lull" full of emptiness once her grown daughter no longer needs her full attention. She has neglected her own needs and interests for so long that she has idea no how to begin to fill the void that has entered her life. But this mother's burden becomes another mother's ticket to freedom in Bette Pesetsky's "Care By Women." The mother of three daughters in this story who fails to make her daughters' lives perfect, as she had intended, revels in her own freedom once they are grown and the opportunity arises for her to build an identity for herself.

A nonconformist daughter's unusual Christmas present helps a frustrated middle-aged mother in Jane Keon's "The Seventh Daughter" begin to find herself. Through the catharsis of expressing herself in writing in the blank books her youngest daughter has given her year after year, the mother in this story begins to expose her true feelings and discover who she really is while she also begins to appreciate and grow closer to her once misunderstood daughter.

Several of the mothers characterized in these narratives are portrayed as intriguing eccentrics. Irene Narell portrays a mother in "Papa's Tea" who is fiercely independent and spontaneous, a noctural person who sneaks her four children to the theater at night after her husband has fallen asleep so that she can watch the late-night feature. The aging mother in Patricia Volk's "The Air of My Youth" decides to cast aside all remnants of her old life and board an airplane bound for Florida, carrying aboard only her pocketbook, to build a new identity for herself. She leaves her two adult daughters with only a "battered envelope" containing their "crumbs of baby teeth" which they bury in the backyard with the bones of a former pet. The daughter of Anna of the Flying Avalons who narrates "The Leap" portrays her mother, once a famous trapeze artist, as a daring young woman who has never lost her courage or balance although she is sightless in her old age.

Conflicting views of mothers and daughters toward gender equality are examined in Joyce Warren's "Fetters." Although the daughter-narrator respects the traditional views of her mother toward women's roles, she develops a more liberated perspective for herself. Unlike her mother, she writes, "I was educated, as my mother was not, to question everything. . ." (8).

SHORT FICTION

213. Antin, Mary. "Malinke's Atonement." America and I: Short Stories by American Jewish Women Writers. Ed. Joyce Antler. Boston: Beacon Press, 1990. 27 – 56.

Although she expresses the belief that daughters are worthless ("a burden on their parents' neck, until they're married off"), the poor Jewish widow in this story depends upon her only daughter's housekeeping skills to manage the household while she works to support her family. The mother pleads for mercy with the rav when her daughter fails to follow his directive. In defense of her daughter's lie that a chicken was kosher after the rav had declared it unclean, Breine Henne argues that her daughter was driven by extreme hunger and perhaps a touch of insanity. Breine Henne also attempts to share the burden of her daughter's guilt by blaming herself for the lie in order to spare her daughter even more grief. But this proves unnecessary, for the rav is compassionate and forgiving of Malinke's waywardness, offering her the opportunity to become educated so that she may have a chance at a better fate in life than her mother has endured as "the egg-woman."

214. Benson, Sally. "Birds in Their Nests Agree." Women and Children First. New York: Random House, 1943. 27 – 31.

Both mother and daughter characterized in this story recognize the void left in the mother's life when her maternal responsibilities are greatly diminished with her daughter's maturation. Widowed as a young mother, Mrs. Armstrong devoted her life to raising her daughter, neglecting her own needs and self-interests. But there was no warning during those full days of motherhood that "one day it would all be over and she would become an elderly lady living in a mediocre suburb with her unmarried daughter" (28). Now that her daughter no longer needs her care, a "deadly lull" full of emptiness has taken over Mrs. Armstrong's life. "It seemed incredible that there was no child to get ready for school, no clock to watch so as to have lunch on the dot, no small clothes to wash. It had never occurred to her while Anna was growing up that a time would come when she herself would have to live with maturity" (28). When Mrs. Armstrong criticizes another mother for leaving her children "to fly around the country" and vows critically that she would never have done such a thing, it is her daughter who expresses her mother's unspoken feelings when she remarks candidly, " 'You might have been better off if you had' " (30).

215. Blackwoman, Julie. "Kippy." Lesbian Fiction: An Anthology. Watertown, MA: Persephone Press, 1981. 77 – 84.

The black daughter who narrates this story has to defend the sexual orientation of her mother against one of the other street kids of West Philly who calls her mother a "bulldagger"—a woman considered a freak because she acts and dresses as if she really wants to be a man. Although Kippy knows her mother is not a bulldagger, but a lesbian who prefers the companionship of women to men and desires to remain a woman, she cannot think of the words to protect her mother and, at the same time, help the other children who are watching the confrontation understand. Feeling disloyal to her mother, Kippy resorts to the threat of violence in self-defense, which intimidates the name-caller and disperses the crowd. Kippy's anger dissolves into laughter following the near-confrontation with the relief that the defense of her mother's reputation has not cost her additional anxiety.

216. Braverman, Kate. "Naming Names." Squandering the Blue." New York: Fawcett Columbine, 1990. 101 – 125.

This narrative is a portrait of adolescent life in west Los Angeles during the 1950s, a life largely shaped by maternal role models. Early in life the children were divided into groups whose mothers did and did not work. "If your mother worked and you lived in an apartment," the narrator writes, "your shame and inadequacy were indisputable" (110). Mothers such as the narrator's worked because their husbands were disabled, dead, or missing. A few of the mothers were divorced. "This was a world where there were still obscenities," the narrator writes. "The word 'divorce' was one of them" (110). These mothers rarely smiled. The first time the narrator saw a woman laugh she was "stunned." They followed much the same dreary routine day after day, coming home from work, "beaten and exhausted." Dinners became a predictable and monotonous faire:

> They know what each dinner will be for the next month. It will be the same. Potatoes, rice, white bread with margarine, hamburger twice a week, oranges, maybe, and in summer, watermelon. We don't have coffee at home. It is too expensive. We drink tap water with sugar in it. Our plates and glasses don't match. We save jars from jam and drink out of them. (111)

The mothers described in Bravermann's narrative have no money for turkeys at Thanksgiving, nor the energy to celebrate. "Who would they invite?" the narrator wonders. "Their blood relatives have decided that they are expendable. They are without family. And there is nothing to be grateful about" (115). Trapped in a "cemetery above ground," these mothers will eventually break down from exhaustion, and someone younger will be rewarded with their jobs.

The daughters of these mothers grow up ashamed and ostracized, wearing mismatched clothes rejected by more fortunate daughters, believing that they will never be able to escape "this limbo of west LA," knowing that they are condemned to poverty and unhappiness. "I am learning attitudes and behaviors it will take me the rest of my life to forget," the narrator confesses (122). The patterns of these mothers' and daughters' lives are dictated by necessity and circumstance, encasing them in a world of miserable impossibility.

217. Carpenter, Carol. "A Fine Day." Iowa Woman. Spring 1982. 14 – 19.

This narrative explores the ambivalent feelings and frustrations of a first-time mother adjusting to the demands of her new role and the unique individuality of her infant daughter. Whenever tiny Amanda's contentment turns into strident cries that cannot be pacified, Ruthie's pleasure and patience gives way to resentment and anger (once she furiously hurls the baby's bottle at a wall when she refuses to drink more) at this new and disruptive intrusion in her life.

218. Coleman, Wanda. "The Seamstress." A War of Eyes and Other Stories. Santa Rosa: Black Sparrow Press, 1988. 39 – 40.

This portrait of a sweatshop worker-by-day, mother-of-four by night from the perspective of her 11-year-old daughter characterizes a woman who sacrifices herself for the needs of her family. The unnamed woman, symbolic of many lower class mothers, labors over a sewing machine eight hours each day to meet the needs of her family, comes home "so tired, baby, I could cry," and relates to her daughter the details of her day because "there is no one else there to listen but me," the narrator writes (40). Despite her fatigue, the mother finds the energy to bend over her own sewing machine to finish a new dress for her daughter to wear. "I wonder as a I watch her," the narrator writes of her mother and her labor with a mixture of price and curiosity. "What must it be like? And what makes her battle it so hard and never give in?" (40).

219. Cooper, J. California. "The Doras." The Matter is Life. New York: Doubleday, 1991. 147 – 227.

This long narrative is a characterization of a mother and her four daughters, as seen through the eyes of Dora's "dearest friend." Dora, "born to a mother who had seen the tail end of slavery," was sent to an orphanage at the age of five because her mother could no longer feed her. Dora ran away ten years later and bore her husband three daughters—Lovedora, Windora, and Endora—before he died. She bore another daughter—Splendora—to a man she never married. "Now, her other daughters didn't like her havin that baby. As they grew up they always counted Splendora as a kind of outsider, you know? Not one of them, cause they knew their father was dead and he couldn't'ta made that baby. As they grew up they sometimes told her she wasn't all part of them. They was jealous of their mother's love for her, too" (165). Although she was single and poor, Dora had high expectations for her daughters, her "Dora dolls," as she called them. A friend remembers Dora's devotion to motherhood:

> She worked hard, hard til she was lookin old early herself. Sun-up to sun-down and some thru the night. She grew old and they grew up. You sure got a job to do if you got four pretty girls to watch over as they growin up. Sides keepin them full and clothed so they don't need nothing from somebody would take advantage of em. Sometimes it's more than two people can handle. Dora had to do it . . . alone. (170).

Through their mutual and love and perseverance, the daughters and their mother survive the hardships and disappointments of life, ranging from sexual abuse to kidney failure, as each daughter pursues an individual dream of her own making, and granddaughters with names such as Pandora and Goldora are born to carry on the Dora tradition.

220. Erdrich, Louise. "The Leap." My Mother's Daughter: Stories by Women. Ed. Irene Zahava. Freedom, CA: The Crossing Press, 1991. 231 – 239.

The daughter of Anna of the Flying Avalons portrays her mother as a dauntless woman who once perfomed daring trapeze feats before her husband died during their infamous blindfold somersault act. "My mother once said," the narrator remembers, "that I'd be amazed at how many things a person can do within the act of falling" (234). The narrator discovered the truth of her mother's words when they jumped together from the window of their flaming home when she was seven years old. "I know that she's right," the narrator remembers. "I knew it even then. As you fall there is time to think" (238).

Now, aging with cataracts that have left her sightless, the narrator's mother moves with "catlike precision" through the house, a skill left over from her earlier trapeze training, "lightly touching her way along walls and running her hands over knickknacks, books, the drift of a grown child's belongings and castoffs," never upsetting an object or losing her balance (231).

221. Freeman, Judith. "What Is This Movie?" Family Attractions. New York: Viking Press, 1988. 113 – 136.

This story contrasts the attitudes of three generations of mothers and daughters toward their relationships with men. While the grandmother learns there is sexual pleasure after retirement and slips comfortably into a relationship that provides much more than the companionship she envisioned, her divorced daughter flounders in her attempt to develop a relationship with a man who will only commit himself in "increments." " 'I don't think I'll ever get it right with men,' " she confesses to her mother, who refuses to become involved in her daughter's complicated affairs (132). The youngest woman of the triad experiences her first, intense adolescent crush on a boy while she nurtures romanticized and surprisingly traditional notions of becoming a housewife and mother, building a "happy home" she has never had. Each woman in this story is better at judging and correcting the lives of the others than she is at managing her own life. " 'I don't know why we all can't just be what we want to be,' " says the granddaughter. " 'We keep trying to make each other over' " (135). This story illustrates the societal changes that have restructured and complicated the relationships of men and women and how these have affected mother-daughter relationships as well.

222. Gerber, Merrill Joan. "Hairdos." Chattering Man. Atlanta: Longstreet Press, 1991. 77 – 84.

While the middle-aged mother characterized in this story laments the passage of her youth and loss of her three daughters to adulthood, her youngest daughter revels in the prospect of beginning college and an independent life, oblivious to her mother's midlife crisis. In the restaurant where the story takes place, the mother wonders aloud to her husband and daughter whether or not she should continue dyeing her graying hair to look younger. She assures herself that while she doesn't "want to give my daughters the message that staying young is everything, neither do I want them to think that I am leaving ths sexual arena entirely" (78). This mother, who keeps diapers in the trunk of her car as souvenirs of days past and envies younger mothers feeding their toddlers in restaurants, regrets not that she doesn't like desserts anymore, but that she misses "wanting" them—another symbol of her youth now past. When she takes a taste of her daughter's dessert and finds herself wanting more, her unexpected pleasure is a reassurance that she has retained at least some of the joys of youth.

223. Giles, Molly. "Self-Defense." Rough Translations. Athens: University of Georgia Press, 1985. 107 – 119.

The 38-year-old single mother who narrates this story begins to recognize her own needs as an individual as she tires of the responsibilities of motherhood and forces her adolescent daughter toward greater independence. As Amanda approaches her eighteenth birthday nursing far-fetched dreams of reveling in her freedom by living in a desert and writing poetry when she has yet to learn to drive an automobile, her mother begins to reevaluate her own life. The mother realizes that she, too, is approaching a new phase of independence and needs to concern herself more with her own life and less with her daughter's. "What will it be like next year if Amanda does leave home?" the narrator wonders. "What will it be like when I'm not 'still tied down'?" (114 – 115). Numerous possibilities begin to enter her mind—quitting an unfulfilling job, beginning a new relationship, finishing a degree, traveling the world. "Yesterday I was seventeen," the narrator remembers. "Tomorrow at this rate, I'll be seventy. Time is going by too fast, and it doesn't seem to be taking me with it" (115). As she begins to reject her daughter's self-centeredness and insist that she accept the responsibilities of an adult, this mother begins to envision herself as an individual with an identity beyond that of an anonymous woman who remains only "somebody's mother."

224. Girion, Barbara. "A Very Brief Season." A Very Brief Season. New York: Charles Scribner's Sons, 1984. 27 – 48.

The daughter in this story learns more about adolescent conformity and the similarities between her mother at an earlier age and herself in this story. Although she and her mother disagree about her need to conform in dress and appearance with other teenagers her age, the daughter gains more respect for her mother's opinions when she learns through her grandmother that her mother was "just as insecure about her looks and style" when she was her age (48). Her grandmother says of adolescence: "I guess it's a special growing up time in the life of a young woman when she feels she's got to be like everybody else, before she's developed her own taste and set of rules. I guess you could say it's a very special brief season. You just have to pass through it on the way to growing up" (47). The narrator begins to understand her own behavior and her mother's concern for her individuality when she realizes that she may be "still caught in the middle of that very brief season" but is almost "ready to pass right through" (48).

225. Grau, Shirley Ann. "The Man Outside." Something in Common: Contemporary Louisiana Stories. Ed. Ann Brewster Dobie. Baton Rouge: Louisiana State University Press, 1991. 199 – 213.

This narrative is a portrait of a woman who for 15 years raised 11 children by herself after her husband "had his vision and stopped working and took his dog and went to live in the little shed down by the spring, right on the east side of the swamp" (202). Never admitting to her children how she felt toward their estranged father, the narrator's mother "kept on bringing his food and bearing his children" (202). "My mother," writes her daughter, "was what you would call a driving woman," a woman of high principles and strict standards for her children, a woman with the ability to stretch limited resources to support her family (200). "For all of her energy, she wasn't a thin woman or a gaunt one," her daughter writes. "She was short, and inclined to be heavy. Her hair changed from light brown to gray, but her face was full and pink. Her mother had been German, and the blood in her showed. Even mud on her looked clean" (202).

226. Grossman, Lynn. "In Proportion." Fiction of the Eighties: a decade of stories from TriQuarterly. Eds. Reginald Gibbons and Susan Hahn. Chicago: Northwestern University, 1990. 397 – 399.

This short narrative examines the mother-daughter relationship in terms of sizes and proportions, constantly shifting with time and experience. When the mother and her eight-year-old daughter unexpectedly encounter death together for the first time, the mother feels ineffectual in proportion to her young daughter. "I am as small as she is when it comes to this," the mother confesses (399). On the day of her daughter's birth, the mother remembers, "I could not imagine a time when I would not be bigger than she was" (399). But as her daughter grows older and matures, the proportions which separate mother and daughter seem less pronounced and predictable to the mother.

227. Inness-Brown, Elizabeth. "Sundays and Holidays. Satin Palms. Canton, NY: Fiction International, 1981. 56 – 61.

This narrative takes place during a mother-daughter luncheon where the daughter attempts to discover the cause of her mother's depression. She learns that not only is her mother suffering from midlife regrets of what her life might have been like if fate had been different but also that she was an unplanned child whose birth has contributed to her mother's lack of self-fulfillment. To the envy of her mother, it seems like her daughter has everything ahead of her in life while her own possibilities seem to be dwindling in comparison. " 'You still have your life out there,' " she explains to her daughter. " 'Thirty-two and not married. No children. No attachments. No chains' " (59).

228. Kauffman, Janet. "My Mother Has Me Surrounded." Places in the World a Woman Could Walk. New York: Alfred A. Knopf, 1983. 3 – 15.

"My mother is not the distinctly drawn mother of magazines; she is not clear-cut," writes the daughter-narrator of this story (19). The Mennonite mother she characterizes is a commanding woman, someone powerful yet sensitive, strong but compassionate. The daughter understands that she is a part of this woman she admires, not ready yet to detach herself and face the world alone. "My mother has me surrounded," she writes. "I must be hers" (21). The daughter realizes, however, that eventually she must break away from her the strength and protection of her mother and establish her own separate identity.

229. Keon, Jane. "The Seventh Daughter." Calyx 3.1 (1990/91): 93 – 99.

A misfit daughter's unconventional Christmas gifts help her mother find an outlet for her frustrations as a misunderstood woman in this story. Through the catharsis of writing, made possible by Martha's gifts, Bernice begins to expose her true feelings and discover who she really is while she begins to understand her once misunderstood seventh daughter for the first time.

While all of Bernice's daughters finished college, Martha dropped out, then returned later to finish a masters degree in "Aquatic Biology, of all things." While all of the other daughers married, Martha married, divorced, and remarried. "Each of the six daughters gave birth to at least two children, except Martha, who adopted a child from Bangladesh" (94). Every Christmas, while other daughters gave their mother crocheted tablecloths, embroidered dresser scarves, and homemade jams, Martha continually gave her mother blank books, which she stored in the attic, unused.

On the day that Bernice determines to throw away the twelve accumulated books ("Why did her daughter continue to give her something for which she'd had no use? And why did she never ask whether or not her mother had used them? Surely her daughter knew she was almost too busy to think her own thoughts, let alone write them down"), she opens one of the books and writes her own name. A flood of words follow, expressing Bernice's irritation as a woman taken for granted and misunderstood by her friends and family. "All of her daughters would be shocked and hurt to read the unsmiling observations, the vicious and sometimes murderous thoughts of their mother," Bernice realizes. "All of them except Martha" (98). But she cannot stop writing. By the time Bernice has filled several books, she mails them to Martha—the seventh, uncharitable, unpredictable—

daughter whom she now realizes is the only one of her daughters who will understand her mother's need to express who she really is on paper.

230. Krysl, Marilyn. "Bondage." Mozart, Westmoreland, and Me. New York: Thunder's Mouth Press, 1985. 117 – 124.

The woman who narrates this story reflects upon her relationship with her mother when she was growing up during post-World War Two as she examines her experiences now that she has become a mother with a daughter of her own. The narrator remembers her mother as a woman of immeasurable energy who made things happy, a woman forever in a frenzy of activity. But her mother was also unhappy, the narrator remembers as early as the age of four, a condition somehow related to her father's return from the war and his propensity to stay on the periphery of action, only occasionally interrupting her mother's progress with irritating demands. Although as a young child the daughter worried that she could be the cause of her mother's unhappiness, she was always sure of the union —"our inevitable linkage"—which bonded her with her mother. It is the same bond which she now shares with her daughter, although her relationship with her own daughter is very different. Although her mother was her primary role model, the circumstances of her life have prevented her from becoming a younger version of her mother. As a single parent, she is always on the go—"busy, impatient, never in any sense of the word a madonna." Although at times she enjoys her role as mother, the narrator confesses that "at times I hate the relentless of responsibilities. There is always something pulling at you." Like her mother "I, too, want things beautiful," she writes, but "there is always one more errand to do on the way home" (122). A picture taken of her mother at the age of 52 stands as proof that she has succeeded in accomplishing her life's goals. "She wears a look of happy triumph: she's made it," the narrator writes. "The pie is cooling, the laundry put away, and there is daylight left. She has accomplished all she intended. The vicissitudes of life have not ground her down. Instead, she rose and came to meet them, each one. Beauty has been brought forth for half a century" (124). The narrator senses that in her own life there will not be such tangible signs of accomplishment, but there will be an enduring bond of closeness she will share with her daughter as she has with her mother.

231. Narell, Irena. "Papa's Tea." The Woman Who Lost Her Names. Ed. Julia Wolf Mazow. New York: Harper and Row, 1980. 49 – 57.

The young narrator of this story portrays her immigrant mother as a woman to whom "life beckoned with irresistible force" (52). A fiercely individualistic, spontaneous woman, her mother sings to the open window "as if all the sound and glory of a spring morning in the country had found its way into our Bronx apartment" (50). Forever smiling, her mind is always on beautiful things, even when there seems to be nothing to be cheerful about. A perfect seamstress, she sews with perfection but keeps such an untidy household, she can never find her own clothes. Once when she expressed a desire to own a mink stole, her daughter recalls, her father joked that she wanted the coat "so she can keep it underneath the washtub" (51). More than once she has forgotten to meet her children home from school for their midday lunch, leaving them locked out in the street, and frequently fails to have her husband's tea prepared for after work. Such neglect is not intentional; her mind is simply preoccupied with other concerns, she loses track of the time. Her mother, the narrator admits, is a noctural person. "Night does things to her," she writes. "Her eyes begin to shine her little feet begin to dance with impatience. She must be off and going somewhere. Sometimes I think that only with the advent of night does mama really begin to realize fully her fierce joy of living" (55). While her husband snores, she sneaks her four children, their pajamas beneath their clothes, to the movie theater where she watches the feature several times until the movie house closes down for the night. "Mama and her movies!" the daughter exclaims (55).

232. Nunez, Sigrid. "The Summer of the Hats." The Pushcart Prize XIV: Best of the Small Presses. Ed. Bill Henderson. Yonkers, NY: Pushcart Press, 1989. 196 – 209.

The adult daughter who narrates this story remembers her mother as a once beautiful woman, savvy about fashion and "passionate" about her appearance, who decided she was no longer young at age 32 and suddenly gave up on life. "The tragedy wasn't being old," the narrator writes, "it was not being young anymore" (200). So closely bonded were mother and daughter during her childhood that the narrator remembers she was "forced to acknowledge once more how utterly dependent my happiness was on hers, a thought that could at different times fill me with anger, tenderness, or fear" (199). Once her mother was convinced she could never be young or attractive again, however, she became self-absorbed in depression and neglected her family. By the time she realized her mistake and resolved to begin living—and mothering—again, she was diagnosed with a terminal illness. The mother in this narrative is characterized by her admiring daughter as a proud woman who could not bear to face the passing of her youth.

233. Paley, Grace. "Other Mothers." Feminist Studies 4.2 (1978) 166 – 169.

In this series of vignettes, the narrator recalls many mothers of differing nationalities and philosophies—Zionists, Communists, Democrats, Socialists—who influenced her development as she was growing up. In the final paragraph of the narrative the daughter, now a mother of two children, evaluates her own performance as a mother. Has she adequately prepared her children to leave home? If they accidentally drop a nickel, will they leave it for a gleaner, as her mother taught her to do? Will they place friendship above competition? She has passed on the socialist ideals and humanitarian values she absorbed from the many mothers who influenced her life. Her narrative pays tribute to a long history of mothers and their maternal philosophiess passed on to yet another generation.

One of the most poignant memories the narrator relives as a daughter was overhearing her relatives talking about her mother's approaching death, a secret which she was not told. During their last years together, the narrator remembers coexisting awkwardly with her mother while the inevitability of her death remained unspoken. "I fear her death," the narrator remembers her childhood feelings. "She is afraid for my life" (169).

234. Pesetsky, Bette. "Care By Women." Stories Up To a Point. New York: Alfred A. Knopf, 1981. 75 – 83.

A mother of three daughters who devotes her maternal energy to trying to make life perfect for her children and fails undergoes a number of personal changes during her midlife in this story. After her grown daughters scatter and her marriage ends, what troubles Mrs. Triton "was not that everything had slipped away but that she could accept its loss, adjust to all these changes. I'm free, she said when no on was around to hear" (82). Mrs. Triton's failure as the perfect wife and mother is her success as an individual as she begins to build her own identity apart from her role as wife and mother.

235. Robison, Mary. "An Amateur's Guide to the Night." An Amateur's Guide to the Night. Boston: David R. Godine, 1989. 15 – 28.

The daughter who narrates this story and her eccentric mother characterized in this story are more like sisters than mother and daughter, the 35-year-old mother often double-dating with her 17-year-old daughter. Anxious at the thought of losing her daughter, the mother misses her high school graduation and tries to admit herself to a psychiatric hospital. But the two are united while watching a late-night Fright Theatre feature, the mother convincing her daughter there is no room in their cozy relationship for the return of her father.

236. Sasaki, R. A. "The Loom." The Loom and Other Stories. St. Paul: Graywolf Press, 1991. 15 – 35.

The Japanese-American mother of four daughters portrayed in this story sheds a rich personal history of past selves when she becomes a mother. So intent is she in becoming the perfect mother that she forgets how to listen to her own emotions and raises four children who hardly know their mother. When forced away from home to visit her grown daughters, the mother becomes excited to experience new adventures and becomes more receptive to new ideas but once she returns home, her daughters are dismayed to find that she is "once again effaced, part of the house almost, in her faded blouse and shapeless skirt, joylessly adding too much seasoned salt to the dinner salad" (30). " 'We seem to lose ground every time,' " one daughter laments to another. " 'We dig her out, then she crawls back in, only deeper' " (32). As the mother ages and her adult daughters come and go, she contentedly sits at her loom, "weaving the diverse threads of life into one miraculous, mystical fabric with timeless care" (35).

237. Segal, Susan. "Weekend." Iowa Woman. Summer 1990: 21 – 27.

A mother's feelings of inadequacy and ambivalence toward first time motherhood are explored with frank realism in this story. "I know I can be a wonderful mother," the narrator confides, "if only the baby will give me a chance" (21). But her daughter shows a decided preference for the babysitter (she rides on Maria's hip while she cleans, the two of them speaking some secret language to each other as they go, "gurgling with pleasure"), and frequently baffles her unprepared mother with prolonged screaming. While the narrator finds occasional pleasure in her daughter's company, her feelings of inadequacy and uncertainty often turn motherhood into a chore to be endured instead of a joy to be savored.

238. Swick, Marly. "Elba." A Hole in the Language. Iowa City: University of Iowa Press, 1990. 1 – 22.

This story examines three generations of mothers and daughters, separated by choice and circumstance, who are about to be reunited. The mother who gave up her home and marriage 24 years ago to guide her daughter through pregnancy and childbirth is now dying of cancer while her daughter, who has now become her primary caregiver, faces the reality of living alone for the first time. But a letter arrives from Texas containing proof that she is not only a mother but a grandmother as well at the age of 40. The young woman in the photograph is unmistakably her own daughter, whom she willingly gave up at birth when she discovered herself pregnant at the age of 16. Before her own mother dies there is still time to reunite great-grandmother, mother, and daughter with newborn son. As the narrator composes a letter inviting the daughter she has never seen to visit, she visualizes the reunion that will take place and inevitably evoke maternal emotions she has never recognized before, as she holds her newborn grandson.

> I breathed in his baby smell of powder and sour milk. I felt his soft warmth, a pleasant weight against my belly, radiating inward. I began to rock, crooning in harmony with the squeaky floorboards, and as I rocked, I began to pile oranges on my lap, one after another, hugging them to me, until my lap was full of oranges, heavy with oranges. And then, for the first time all night, I felt something. It could have been the avalanche of oranges, shifting in my lap, but it felt more like it was on the inside, more like something under the skin, something moving there inside me. (22)

239. Thompson, Sandra. "The Birthday Party." Close-Ups. Athens: University of Georgia Press, 1984. 93 – 98.

The occasion of her daughter's sixth birthday is a time for contemplation for the mother characterized in this story. While her daughter anxiously awaits her guests, the narrator sits admittedly "terrified." "Parties are revealing," she writes, "and I fear what I might learn this year" (94). While her daughter shows signs of growing out of childhood, she thinks of her 87-year-old grandmother who is nearing the end of life. Somewhere between the two she stands, a woman in the midst of divorce facing single-parenthood by herself, both exhilarated by the occasion of her daughter's party and very uncertain about the future of her life.

240. Volk, Patricia. "The Air of My Youth." All It Takes. New York: Atheneum, 1990. 55 – 61.

This story explores the sensations of a daughter reacting to her mother's decision to cast aside her old life, move, and build a new identity. "Ma is going to start out complete new in Florida," the narrator writes. "Her idea is to get on a plane with no luggage, only her pocketbook and cosmetic case, and move into a completely new house. There she will furnish from scratch, down to the teaspoons" (55). "It's her last house," her daughter writes, "and she wants it to have nothing from the past" (58). The only relic of the past the mother offers her adult daughers is a "battered envelope" full of "crumbs of baby teeth" she has kept over the years, which they bury in the backyard with the bones of a former pet, envisioning what conclusions future archaeologists might draw from this odd assortment.

Although the daughters long to inherit some of the family treasures and relics of their childhood, their mother insists on selling everything in the house while excluding her daughters as potential buyers. " 'I could never take money from my children,' " she tells them as she rejects their offers. The narrator still recalls familiar smells from the past associated with her childhood and adolescence spent in this house, but she is left with nothing tangible to symbolize her relationship with her mother, who has made the decision to leave all of her past behind to strangers while she searches for a new identity for herself.

241. Warren, Joyce. "Fetters." The Underground Banquet and Other Stories. Boston: Rowan Tree Press, 1988. 7 – 15.

"Fetters" is a daughter's characterization of a mother who was "tiny, ancient, sparkling, and as resilient as a pocket-sized trampoline," yet very traditional in her outlook on gender equality (7). "I was educated, as my mother was not," writes the daughter-narrator, "to question everything, including social mores, and the result was that she and I argued a great deal. I thought her fettered, and she thought me adrift. I was appalled by the lack of opportunity offered her as a girl to pursue a career: she was equally appalled by the idea that marriage and a family might not offer career enough" (8). The class structure which governed her mother's youth changed drastically by the time her daughter grew up. Yet her mother's attitudes did not follow current trends. A "devoted and doting wife," Frances Leigh "saw as her role in life to make every man she met feel appreciated and admired" (12). To attempt consciousness raising with her mother, admits the narrator, would have been a hopeless endeavor. Mother and daughter come to a loving but definite impasse in their views toward sexual equality, the mother clinging to her familiar fetters, the daughter refusing to be restrained by them.

242. Zelver, Patricia. "Love Letters." A Man of Middle Age and Twelve Stories: New York: Holt, Rinehart and Winston, 1980. 190 – 202.

An adolescent daughter gains respect for her middle-aged mother in this story when she learns that her mother once received love letters written by servicemen during World War Two. Rebecca, who has changed her name several times in order to establish a new identity, considers her mother a dull woman who belongs to a strangely different age of the past, a woman in need to cosmetic surgery to hide the lines of aging (195). Rebecca-Maxine spends most of her time lying on the living room couch "waiting for something to happen. So far, nothing has. There is the implication that I am to blame," writes her mother (192). "I have taken up French and Yoga to escape her," the narrator confesses. "Proper breathing, my Yoga teacher says, is the Answer to Everything" (193). But when Rebecca's aunt sends her love letters written to her mother by soldiers during the war, Rebecca is suddenly "filled with respect, with awe—for me!" exclaims her mother. "I am no longer a Wimp. I have lived!" (202). Although Rebecca's mother weeps, recognizing that the woman addressed in these letters—"The Prettiest Girl in the World," "An Honest-to-God Glamour Girl," "Sweetheart of the Ninety-first"—was not she but a phantom in the imaginations of lonely, frightened, young men, Rebecca nourishes romantic visions of a new image of her mother as a desirable woman.

Sources:

Kisner, Kathleen. "Elegant Oddballs." Rev. of An Amateur's Guide to the Night, by Mary Robison. Belles Lettres. Summer 1991: 37.

Author Index

Authors are listed alphabetically by last name. Numbers refer to bibliographic entries of short stories.

Title Index

Numbers refer to bibliographic entries of short stories.

Subject Index

Numbers refer to bibliographic entries of short stories.

About the Compiler

SUSANNE CARTER is an education specialist with the Western Regional Resource Center of the University of Oregon. Her previous book is *War and Peace through Women's Eyes: A Selective Bibliography of Twentieth-Century American Women's Fiction* (Greenwood, 1992).